MANNERS IN A DIGITAL WORLD

MANNERS IN A DIGITAL WORLD

LIVING WELL ONLINE

DANIEL POST SENNING

INTEGRATED MEDIA

NEW YORK

CONTENTS

ACKNOWLEDGMENTS

The Emily Post Institute is both a five-generation family business and, truly, a team affair. This book is possible due to the invaluable support and input of the entire team. It is with deep appreciation that I thank the following people for their contributions.

Peter and Tricia Post for their patient guidance and editorial assistance through all the phases of producing this book.

Jeanne Martinet for her editorial expertise as well as her good humor.

Gabrielle Dunn for applying her keen eye to the technical details of the new frontier covered in this book.

Anna Post and Elizabeth Howell for their willingness to get down in the trenches and play a critical role in finding the etiquette advice that is the beating heart of this book.

ACKNOWLEDGMENTS

Katherine Cowles, my book agent, for guiding me through the development of the first e-book tackled at the Emily Post Institute.

All the friends and family who contributed stories and thoughtful perspectives to the topic. I hear their unique voices in every page of this book.

And finally my mother, Cindy Post Senning, whose influence is quite simply the foundation of this work.

FOREWORD

Over the last several years, I've had the opportunity to watch my cousin Dan delve into all things technology. For a year, he spent a few hours a day with headphones on, watching Joomla tutorials to learn how to build us a new website. He then single-handedly built that site, complete with all the bells and whistles it needs to support the 150,000-plus unique visitors who drop by each month looking for answers to their etiquette questions. And the site is ever-evolving; I'll never forget the look of satisfaction on his face the day he worked the bugs out of the mobile version of our website. Web ads, analytics, e-newsletters—Dan's digital fingerprints are all over the online world of Emily Post.

What's even more impressive, at least to me, is his baby, *The Etiquette Daily*. EtiquetteDaily.com is a WordPress blog we started several years ago. Before then, we let visitors to our website ask us their burning etiquette questions over e-mail—we even made it easy with a big Ask Us a Question button. And ask they did, to the tune of hundreds of questions each month. This Dear Abby–type service was costing us quite a pretty penny, as we had to pay "Emily's Army," a stalwart group of freelance writers we had trained to answer these questions. In addition, the e-mail response process was technically cumbersome to manage. Leading a team, Dan built *The Etiquette Daily* from the ground up in response—no more "ask us" button. Instead, we post one question and answer a day. But it's the comments and the open threads that really give it life. The community that has sprung up on the site is vibrant, and is growing by leaps and bounds even as I type this.

But it wasn't just our advice that brought them back (great though it is). Dan worked hard to foster that community, engaging with new commenters, defusing spats, and investing die-hard users with community moderator status. This more than anything tells me that he gets at a deep level how vital the human factor behind technology is.

It's funny, because Dan lives in a cabin on the side of a mountain. The kind you have to cross a footbridge to get to. The kind that doesn't get cell reception. So I guess in a way it's no surprise that the Internet is his lifeline there when he isn't hanging with friends by a bonfire or going for hikes with his dog, Magpie. Dan is a fan of the phrase "early adopter" and is constantly looking toward the next new thing. From using new apps to give him a leg up with his fantasy football team to being first in line when the iPad hit the market, he is always a step ahead.

So it makes a lot of sense to me that he would write this book. As a tech-savvy early adopter, he's the perfect candidate to blaze a trail for the Emily Post Institute into the world of e-books. That said, tech savvy isn't enough. It's all well and good to know your way around code, but to talk about the influence technology has on relationships requires other skills, skills Dan has been building by teaching business etiquette seminars for all kinds of industries around the country. Technology and how it affects business relationships takes the cake for the topic most requested by our seminar clients, so it's a subject he's gotten very good at articulating to a variety of audiences. Dan also gained experience framing etiquette questions while writing and editing as one of my coauthors on *Emily Post's Etiquette*, 18th edition. But for his first solo flight, a focused look at technology and how it helps and hinders our relationships couldn't be a more perfect topic.

It's a subject near and dear to my own heart. I've worked with Intel since 2009, talking with media about how mobile devices are affecting our relationships. It's been fascinating following the survey data over the years—most notably an interesting correlation between how often people wish others had better digital manners and how often they admit to using bad ones themselves. Contradictory? Sort of. It tells me we're still at a point of change. We're still figuring out which digital manners we need, and learning the consequences of living without them. This etiquette anarchy won't go on forever, though, and it's books like this one, with advice from someone as uniquely positioned as Dan, that will help firm up the shifting sands beneath our feet—just in time for us to put our heads (and hard drives) in the Cloud.

Anna Post

Burlington, Vermont

July 2012

INTRODUCTION

No medium since the telephone has so radically redefined human communication as the Internet has. Every new communication technology that comes along has to be absorbed by society—and each generates some friction as we find its place in our lives. Just as questions were raised about answering the telephone during dinner decades ago, so too is texting at the table under the microscope now. As new communication platforms and devices continue to launch, this book will help people figure out how to use them to impact their relationships positively. *Manners in a Digital World* is for technophiles and technophobes alike; it's for anyone who wants to navigate today's communication environment with emotional intelligence. Protecting and fostering relationships will be our overarching goal. After all, the whole purpose behind social media and smart, new mobile devices is to connect us to the people we are—or want to be—in relationships with. Business contacts, significant others, friends, and family: how we interact with them through these networks and digital devices matters.

To write about digital media is to take aim at a moving target. Our media and communication environment is changing faster and more dramatically than at any other time in our history. At the same time, *how* people use that technology to connect and interact with others stems naturally from their offline relationships—at least, it should. When it comes to the people factor, we aren't reinventing the wheel. No matter the device or network in question, it is the human relationships behind it that should ultimately be served by communication tools, both new and old.

And there are so many kinds of relationships and interactions. I'll cover how the whole family interacts on Facebook and photo-sharing sites—both kids and grandparents alike. Photo sharing itself is a huge topic. The etiquette of tagging and posting raises questions about what's respectful, and whether to ask permission before posting. Facebook, Twitter, LinkedIn—I'll take a look at the major sites and their manners subcultures. Online gaming is one of the biggest Internet communities around, with its own rules of engagement. Dating is fast on its heels, though, and we'll talk about the art of finding love online. Never far from anyone's mind (thanks to that smartphone!) is work. Navigating job interviews that might pull up your Facebook page right then and there and avoiding accidental Twitter overshares are just a few of the things that are part of what it means to assess and be smart about digital appropriateness in the workplace today.

This is not a technical "how to" book. It's a book that will give perspective and confidence to both the novice user and the technophile alike. I'll examine the mobile devices people use to communicate (smartphones, tablets, laptops), the social networking platforms they do it through (Facebook, Twitter, LinkedIn), and the ways our relationships are affected by both. I will offer strategies for navigating these purposefully—how to make choices that build a good experience for everyone involved—and highlight some of the most common trouble areas so they can be avoided in the first place. Ultimately, we are talking about traditional social norms—being friendly, thoughtful, considerate, sincere, respectful—and how we carry those with us when we enter the world of social media and mobile devices.

1

NETIQUETTE

We love our mobile devices. We love our Facebook, Tumblr, and Twitter accounts. No one can dispute that the Internet has—in just a few short years—reshaped the way we live our lives. From finding old classmates on Facebook to using FaceTime for reading bedtime stories to our kids back home when we're on business trips, we are more instantly connected than ever before. Gone are the village well and the water cooler as the places to get the latest news; now information—from wedding photos to tweets about breaking international news—is shared and consumed from the palm of our hands. All this connecting can help us to do what matters most in etiquette: build and support the relationships that matter to us.

Unfortunately, nearly every day there is another headline illustrating the latest example of bad cyberspace or mobile-device behavior. Personal e-mails are sent to the entire company. Phones go off during concerts and movies—

even worship services. People insist on talking about the most personal topics in the grocery line, on the train, or at work. Embarrassing videos depicting egregiously bad behavior are posted on YouTube and spread through social networks like wildfire. Maybe we are seeing more outrageous behavior than ever before because we are recording more of it and sharing it with more people than was possible even just a few short years ago. Certainly the glut of digital information often leaves us dazed and confused, and worse, overwhelmed and filterless.

Obviously we value manners, or we wouldn't feel so aggrieved at how frequently they are ignored. I often take calls from reporters wanting my comments on the perceived decline of manners in an increasingly digital world. I see what they're getting at, and the numbers are there: One recent study showed that nearly three-quarters of Americans think that mobile-device manners are getting worse, and the same study showed that one in five people excuses his or her own bad behavior because "everyone is doing it." I think it's the rare person who hasn't been offended by someone's bad tech manners (be it from a smartphone or a social network) at some point.

But this book debunks the myth that there are no manners to be found in today's mobile communication environment. Sure there are bad manners, but there are good ones too. Take the very word "etiquette." From the French for "little signs," it also connotes "social rules" both in French and in English. In fact, the two meanings share a history. King Louis XIV of France needed to give his nobles a bit of help behaving properly at his palace at Versailles, so little signs were posted telling them what was what—social dos and don'ts for dummies, so to speak. It's been fascinating to watch new "etiquettes"—little signs—that tell us how to act showing up in response to bad mobile behavior. At the pharmacy, at the gym, in restaurants, at salons, at banks—they're everywhere: "No cell phones, please."

Beyond the signs from management, there are self-imposed rules as well. Most people know not to take a phone call right in the middle of a meeting (or at least to step outside first) and to send a text instead of making a phone call to tell a friend you're running late. Even reaching for a smartphone to settle a debate at a dinner party about which film was Clint Eastwood's directorial debut is frowned on (unless your dinner companions ask you to).

Rapidly developing technologies and new ways of communicating can challenge long-established social norms—such as not interrupting a meeting or bugging your fellow diners. However, the fundamental rules that guide all good social interactions still apply no matter what medium connects two people: Treat others with respect. Think about how your actions will affect the people around you. Be considerate of the feelings of those you interact with. Whether it is a blog or a smartphone, the degree to which new media help us build and sustain our relationships depends entirely on how well we use it.

Anna Post, my cousin and a business etiquette trainer at the Emily Post Institute, has built an effective teaching moment into her corporate seminars when she talks about the best ways to use a smartphone. She takes out her phone, the latest and coolest device on the market, and holds it up in the air. "This is my phone," she announces. "It is not rude; it is not polite. It's just a phone. It's how I use it that could be rude or courteous." This demonstration is a very simple, clear, and personal way to illustrate the heart of the matter: thinking about how using any piece of technology will affect other people is the key to using it well.

> ## A Short History of Netiquette
>
> The word "netiquette" (from "network" and "etiquette") has been in use since at least the early 1980s, back in the simple days of a primarily text-based web network linking schools and research institutions. Hard-core etiquette fans and technophiles might enjoy Brad Templeton's USENET blog Dear Emily Postnews (www.Templetons .com/brad/emily.html#emily). He is credited not only with suggesting the idea of the "dot" used everywhere in web addresses, but also, some say, with coining the term "netiquette."

NICENESS

Let's take it offline for a minute. Niceness, also known as good manners, speaks to behaviors we describe as civil, "being cool about something," "doing the right thing," or being appropriate for the time, place, or company we are in. The word "etiquette" technically sums it up, but frankly, it can sound old-fashioned.

Offline, basic niceness is about treating those around us with consideration, respect, and honesty. We don't have to pretend to be someone's best friend, and we don't have to smile sweetly if insulted. But we do have to be in control of our own actions, and we have a responsibility to act respectfully toward others.

This is no great leap forward, and although a great deal of our technology is brand-new, the socialization that occurs through it is not. While the digital world has opened new ways to socialize and new ways to expand a social circle, the interaction is as old as two people getting together to talk about the best way to start a fire from two sticks and some leaves. We are social creatures, and digital devices and platforms just give us new ways to do the same old things. We talk to one another. We connect. We do business. We meet new people. We fall in love.

RUDENESS

Without the check of a reproachful glance, people can be unkind and inconsiderate, as well as frustratingly anonymous. Most people don't set out to offend, but because everyone is more connected than ever before and because almost everyone has a camera-equipped phone, the unintended offense can reach far and wide. Technology makes communication so easy, immediate, and convenient—available anywhere, from airline seats to toilet seats—that it unfortunately also makes it just as easy and immediate to be unintentionally rude. We all know how easy it is to pass on a negative story, complaint, or sometimes even just a bad feeling. On the web these instances have the potential to be shared and amplified, turning ripples into waves. When we have access to so much information about one another all of the time, it's easy to forget the boundaries we should keep.

There's no question that the immediacy of communication causes stress: "I need that report now!" "Did you get the e-mail?" "I just read the verdict—didn't you?" "Are you in the loop?" It's eight thirty p.m. and your boss is calling—again. Immediacy can be convenient, and it can also be overwhelming. Instead of thinking, we often just react.

Generational perspective can be another point of friction. Ask a room full of

Americans if they think we are ruder today than twenty or thirty years ago, and a solid majority of hands will go up. (I do this at the start of every business seminar I teach.) We all easily fall prey to the feeling that society is slipping. And yet every generation throughout history has felt this way. What we learn when we are young becomes our "normal," our standard. But society and its norms, social codes, and manners move on as times change. New social codes emerge, and old ones disappear as they outlive their utility. Knowing where you are in this shifting landscape is part of figuring out the best ways to behave. It can feel as though today's cascade of digital information is washing away the manners of the past, but it is just redefining the coastline a bit. Keep your wits about you and you may even find a wave or two to catch and ride to higher ground!

Our Brave New World

The Internet and mobile devices have changed the fabric of our lives. Many of the ways digital communication has affected daily living are so pervasive it can be hard to remember that we used to live without them. I think these are some of the best things about life online.

- Need to know something or how to do something? The Google search is a new norm for finding out anything instantly. Wikipedia.com has replaced the *Encyclopaedia Britannica,* no longer in print as of 2012, as the repository of the world's collective knowledge; and Ask.com is currently the largest of the ask-the-Internet-a-question knowledge aggregators. It is simply amazing the answers that are out there waiting.

- Want to track personal finances or follow the markets? Yodlee.com and Mint.com

---

are powerful, personal, free finance tools, and finance.Yahoo.com and money.CNN.com are two of the many excellent market-tracking financial portals.

- Got the travel bug? Check your route or make your own custom maps with Google Maps. Book travel at Travelocity.com, Orbitz.com, or at the website of your favorite discount airline. If you're craving some adventure, try the online Lonely Planet travel guides or even a house-share system like HomeExchange.com.

- Time to enjoy a movie or listen to the radio? No trip to the video store or playing with rabbit ears required. Netflix, Pandora, and now Spotify have come to the rescue!

- Tired of the evening news? Every major news outlet from the broadcast networks to cable channels streams content online. For that matter, so do major papers and leading news outlets all over the world. Why not customize a personal evening news program out of the best sources your web has to offer?

- Like to do things yourself? You can build your own websites for free at WordPress.com and find out more about how this is really possible at WordPress.org. Believe it or not, the Internet is full of smart, caring, creative people. The open-source communities that develop and share software collectively, like the one that developed WordPress and the Mozilla Firefox browser, are some of the great resources of the online world.

- Don't like paying bills or running errands? While you can't avoid them completely, it can take less time to make your bill payments online. To save time and aggravation, shop online or check availability and sales at local vendors before you venture out. In some areas, free home delivery is even an option. Amazing!

The Good, the Bad, and the Ugly

When it comes to new technology and digital manners, we have all experienced the good, the bad, and the ugly. Some aspects of new technology allow us to really shine and be our best, most engaged, selves—the good. There are other aspects that seem to encourage and even amplify bad behaviors and tendencies—the bad. And then there are all the things that have no specific human intention behind them but that can nonetheless have a significant negative influence on how we feel and act—the ugly. I'm thinking in terms of the spaghetti western film of the same name, from Italian director Sergio Leone. The world is more complicated than just black and white, good and evil. His film is a comedic wink that life isn't so simple and clear. You'll need a little half-smile on your face to confront life's inevitable complexities. And it's just as true in the digital Wild, Wild West.

The Good

Let's not forget that new technology can be a vehicle for the very best manners. Not the first thing that comes to mind? A connected world provides more opportunities to be courteous and considerate, not fewer. For example:

- A teen uses her phone to call her parents when plans change, because she doesn't want anyone to worry.

- A client unexpectedly writes a glowing recommendation of you on your LinkedIn profile.

- A friend stuck in traffic calls to say he'll be late.

- A colleague Googles "Jewish religious services" before visiting a synagogue for the first time with a new friend from work.

- A couple sets up a wedding website to help coordinate travel information for the guests who are attending their dream wedding in Hawaii.

THE BAD

But of course with the good comes the bad. Just as new communication technology presents opportunities for good manners and building relationships, it also allows for some truly egregious behavior. Think . . .

- A coworker so engrossed in personal calls, IM chats, and beating the next level on Angry Birds that he completely forgets to reply to the client who was waiting to hear from him

- The person in the waiting room chatting on a phone, sharing the intimate details of her recent gallbladder surgery

- A commuter who is texting while driving and doesn't notice a semi-truck has moved into his lane

- The Facebook friend who posted a picture from her bachelorette party that was best left on the hard drive

THE UGLY

Nothing's perfect, including the latest mobile device, gadget, or app. There are certain aspects of our new media landscape that, although annoying, are part and parcel of where communication technology is at today. They can be incredibly frustrating, and sometimes even feel like personal slights, but in reality have little to do with the behavior of the people using them. We can learn to minimize and live with them, but they are not going to disappear, however well we act or well intentioned we may be. Learning to deal well with these technical foibles is part of operating with any grace in this brave new world.

- Dropped calls and endless software updates are so common that they are simply accepted as daily frustrations in the digital universe.

- Autocorrect texting and e-mail errors have even become a source of great humor, and depending on the error, great embarrassment.

- The hilarious Facebook quiz your friend just took requires you to give the app permission to access all of your personal information.

- Answering purse- or butt-dial calls from a friend whose phone calls you more than he does loses its appeal quickly.

These ugly, communal badland experiences litter the rough-and-tumble, Wild-West digital communication terrain. To truly enjoy the benefits of cutting-edge new tools we need to understand and accept their limitations, and then remember to be patient with people when we're inconvenienced by something that may not be their fault or intention.

Emily Post: Early Adopter

Calling cards, telegraph, telephones, radio, television, fax machines, answering machines, pagers, cell phones, video calling, smartphones. What would Emily Post think? Emily was a fan of technology. There are a few old family videos of Emily giving a tour of her Martha's Vineyard home and office, showing off her state-of-the-art radios. As the host of one of the nation's most popular radio programs in the 1930s, she was enthralled with the idea that her voice was beamed into living rooms all across the country through the miracle of modern science. In fact, she had a radio in every room.

Emily was not just tolerant of new technology, she was an early adopter. She would lie in repose on her daybed and record her thoughts on a first-generation Dictaphone for her assistant to transcribe later. In fact, she loved it so much that she named it Suzy.

IT'S ALL ABOUT RELATIONSHIPS

No matter where you live, how old you are, or what language you speak, you have some combination of friends, family, loves, and/or coworkers in your life. Digital communications have the potential to affect all of these fundamental relationships, and we want to get it right. When we are trying to figure out the best way to use a new device or the best way of communicating, the answer always depends on what's best for the people involved. Is it the right way to get in touch with the person? Texting my grandfather probably won't get me anything but a confused phone call, so I might as well call first and skip the confusion. And the girl I just met at the coffee shop—no "maybe we could hang out sometime" e-mail for her; face-to-face is the best way to impress her when asking her out on a date. But it's also about the people who aren't in my personal sphere. I have a relationship with them to honor as well, so I'll step away from the crowded gate area to check in with a client. This approach—thinking about how my actions will affect relationships—can be employed again and again to decipher what the best digital manner is for any situation that could arise, now or in a 3.0 world.

IF ONLY COMMON SENSE WERE COMMON

When the advice on manners I teach at seminars or provide in media interviews at the Emily Post Institute elicits the response "Well, that makes sense," or "That sounds like common sense," I know I've done my job. Manners should make sense in relation to the way we really live—they can't just be arbitrary, archaic, or esoteric rules for their own sake. So, if the behaviors that I describe as embodying good manners seem so intuitive that their application to a given situation is a natural fit, I know I have identified fundamentally useful material.

And why do we need to spend time stating the obvious, so to speak? Because despite the elegantly simple solutions to most etiquette situations—take responsibility, think about the people around you, act in ways to make things easier for others—bad behavior persists. Put simply, people don't always do what appears obvious and correct to those around them. Someone has a bad day and therefore feels their rudeness is justified, or doesn't make the effort to use what they know is good behavior. Getting past the laziness and lack of awareness and excuses that precede a rude act takes practice. It needs to happen again and again until the right behavior becomes habit. Good behavior is achieved by continuing to remind and reaffirm and act in ways that overcome the tendency to put ourselves before the people around us. Make a mistake despite your best efforts? Try, try again. Much of what I will suggest as best practice and good behavior in this book should sound intuitive once you stop to think about it. I certainly hope so anyway!

NETIQUETTE TODAY: THE GOOD NEWS

So where are we now? In a world where people know how they want to be treated but don't always get it, figuring out the best ways to behave sets you apart. Technology now lets you reach out to new business contacts on LinkedIn that you'd never have had access to before. It allows you to have relationships with far-flung fifth-grade best friends and long-lost second cousins you'd never stay in touch with otherwise. And via blogs and tweets and social-network groups, you can form meaningful connections with people you may never even meet in person. You can do all these things and more, but you have to do them well and you have to do them appropriately to get the most out of them. Rather than feel overwhelmed by this thought, there is tremendous empowerment not only in the access you have to new people, but also in how you choose to structure your interactions. Don't like the tone of a community? You don't have to join it. Wish someone had replied to your post? Reply to theirs instead. Modeling the behavior you'd like to see in the digital world puts you in the driver's seat. Ultimately, you get to decide how you will act and build your relationships. And the benchmarks for that behavior are the same fundamental principles that Emily Post applied to human interactions back in her day—treating people with honesty, respect, and consideration.

2

MOBILE DEVICES

My sixty-eight-year-old father used to be a chronic mobile-phone borrower. He was the last one in the family to get his own and he resisted this new technology until it practically wasn't new anymore. Don't get me wrong; he programmed computers for more than thirty years and has no trouble mastering technology. His concerns have to do with all the real-people interactions made possible by this modern marvel. He worries that the ladies at his church will be able to reach him more easily with volunteer requests that he simply can't seem to turn down. (It is sometimes easier to be unreachable than to say no.) The thought of my mother's grocery requests chasing him while on his favorite bike ride puts a furrow in his brow. His concerns, while entertaining, are understandable.

Behind our pocket computers and touch-screen tablets is a very real web of human interaction. It's not just clearing the technical hurdles that is the key to success with these devices, it's learning the ways in which their use affects our relationships. I find those interpersonal issues so much more important and interesting.

There are numerous studies that show the public's desire for increased awareness of mobile etiquette. While mobile devices such as iPhones, Black-Berrys, Androids, iPads, Kindles, and laptops come with instructions and help departments, human relationships do not. If I could tell you only one thing about mobile manners, it would be this: focus on the person or people you are with rather than the tantalizing device in your pocket. Let's first explore the manners associated with how we should use mobile devices, and then take a look at manners that address when and where we should use them (since they are, after all, mobile), as there are a few places where they are more likely to cause annoyance than others.

MOBILE MANNERS FOR MOBILE DEVICES

By the mid-1990s, the Emily Post Institute was awash in complaints about the impolite use of mobile phones. From phones on the dinner table, ringing phones in movie theaters, and bosses calling employees at all hours of the night, the mobile phone created a wave of rudeness not witnessed in decades. The public outcry was loud: mobile users need to use better manners. Keep in mind, society's irritation with the mobile phone isn't with the device, it's with the thoughtless ways the device is used.

TOP TEN MOBILE MANNERS FOR MOBILE DEVICES

Relatively quickly, standards emerged for polite mobile-device use in public. Here's the list of best-practice behaviors we've developed at the Emily Post Institute:

1. Be present. Give your full attention to the people you are with. No matter how well you think you can multitask, don't talk on the phone when you are with other people—whether at a meal, on a date, in a house of worship, or at a coffee shop.

2. Before making a call in public ask yourself if it might be annoying to anyone else—if it would be, step aside first.

3. If you are waiting for a call to coordinate meeting up with people, be sure your phone is on, powered up, and gets a signal. It's so annoying to try to reach someone who is not answering his phone when he should be.

4. Volume is a big contributor to mobile device–related stress, so keep your voice, phone rings, games, music, and videos turned down. Even with headphones, volume can still bug those around you, especially on an airplane or subway.

5. Keep voice messages brief and specific. Remember you are mobile, so it might make sense to include your location along with the time you called.

6. Turn off, or completely silence (this means no "vibrate" mode), your phone when it would be disruptive. Meetings, meals, and movies are

three great times to practice this. Remember, even the light from the phone's display can be distracting in a dark movie theater.

7. Leave your phone behind occasionally. Practice cutting the cord to help you bring your full attention to the activity at hand. Do you really need your phone in class or at a job interview?

8. Be a respectful audience member to performers and those around you at the theater and other live performances. Turn off your device, or at least set it to silent and step outside to check a message or return a call.

9. Some places should stay private: Don't use a mobile phone while using a public restroom (or any restroom). It's awkward for those around you, and makes people wonder about your sense of decency. It's also likely to be awkward for the person on the other end of the line.

10. Practice what you preach. If you don't care for others' poor mobile behavior, don't do those things yourself.

Don't Call from the Stall

Do not, I repeat, *do not,* use your mobile device while you are in shared restrooms (or any restroom, for that matter). As the person talking to you, I do not want to hear those noises, much less the flushing of the toilet. "I'll wait until I'm finished talking to flush," you say. And how do you control other noises in the room or prevent the person in the stall nearby from being subjected to your call? Using the phone while in the restroom is like bringing the person on the other end of the line into the room and is discomfiting to many people.

Finally, the built-in camera is reason enough to put a phone away while you are in the restroom. Please remove even the hint of a possibility that you could be taking a picture of me by not having your phone in your hand while you are in the restroom.

WHO GETS YOUR NUMBER?

When I first got a mobile phone, learning to use it well was a process. In my enthusiasm, I gave my number to everyone. I began to dread the ring because the list of people contacting me was not necessarily the group of people I wanted to be talking to on a regular basis. Does your mobile number get printed on your business card? Is it on your e-mail signature? Your Facebook page? Think about the implications before you decide to include it. For me, a big part of learning to use a mobile phone was simply learning the best ways to distribute my contact information only to those with whom I actually wanted to speak. Being careful about who has your number is more important than I realized at the time.

PHONE CALLS

Some of us just can't seem to let a ringing, buzzing, vibrating, or singing phone lie. We're programmed from a very young age to "answer the phone!" But just because you often carry a phone does not mean you are available to everyone all of the time.

A Zen monastery in California instituted a mindfulness practice around a newly installed phone system. Every time a bell rings at the monastery, including any phones, everyone who hears it says a prayer for peace before they act and respond. The idea is to insert a moment of intentional contemplation before making a habitual response. There is a valuable lesson in this example. The next time your phone rings, before you jump to answer it, pause for just a moment to break the habit of automatically reaching for your phone every time it chimes.

There are times we want to set limits on the mobile phone calls we receive. Do I have to answer if my boss calls at ten p.m.? This one really depends. Know what's generally expected of everyone in your office, and then be consistent. If you feel eight p.m. is a fair boundary, don't pick up at ten p.m. or encourage attempts to contact you at this hour. On the other hand, if you knew constant availability was part of the job you signed up for, then yes, you need to pick up. Then, the next day, ask to have a conversation with your boss to clarify expectations.

VOICE MESSAGES

Some people have stopped leaving voice messages on mobile phones altogether, assuming people will call them back when they see a missed call. Many people find listening to voice messages annoying, and forgo leaving them for others for just this reason. But on the flip side, not everyone is a fan of this. A common complaint is "My friend never listens to my voice mails, she just calls me back and says 'What's up?' Isn't this rude?" Sort of. While it would be nice if she took the extra minute to be prepared for the call, it's not worth making a fuss about if it didn't change the outcome. If listening first would have made a difference, that's worth pointing out with a polite request to please check the voice mail first in the future. Many people simply see that you called and figure they'll skip the message and get to the call. In a way you can be flattered—they don't need a reason to call you back, they just automatically do it when they see you've called. While we can't all be Zen monks, this is a perfect chance to be the good example. Model the behavior you'd like to see in others by listening to voice messages before replying, but let it go when someone else doesn't. The one exception would be business calls; in this case, take a note from the Boy Scouts' motto and always "Be Prepared." Better to know what your boss wants to discuss than to call and say "What's up?" and sound like an idiot.

TEXTING

Texting is simply sending short written messages from one phone or mobile device to another. Millions are sent each day. From an etiquette perspective, the best thing about texting is that you can get a message to someone without having their phone ring at an inopportune time.

Text messaging is a casual communication. It's most effective when used to provide a quick update. Don't use it to inform someone of sad news, confidential or complex business matters, or to have any kind of conversation that should be handled face-to-face.

While it is true that sending a text while on the train is vastly preferable to making a phone call, in many places this substitution won't work. Take one more look at the list of top mobile manners on page 21–22. These rules also apply to texting. What's great about texting is that you can be lost in the aisles of Home Depot and locate your spouse quickly with a text. As your colleague is setting up the room, you can let her know the cord she needs for the presentation will be there in thirty seconds. Here are a few etiquette guidelines unique to texting.

TEXTING DOS AND DON'TS

- Don't assume everyone has unlimited texting as part of their service plan. Check before you text someone excessively or get mad about how rarely they reply.

- Do keep it short. Don't send a novel about what you did last night. If it's going to be more than a few sentences, pick up the phone.

- Do be aware of gut-buster autocorrect spelling mistakes. Visit DamnYouAutocorrect.com if you need proof.

- Don't use elaborate text speak and abbreviations with people who aren't likely to know what they mean.

- Do have fun . . . but don't forget to pick up the phone and call or meet face-to-face for coffee once in a while too.

INSTANT MESSAGE (IM)

IMing is just like texting except that the sending and receiving happens through a service over the Internet instead of through the phone company. Many people use IM features (such as BlackBerry's messaging feature, often referred to as BBMing) through their mobile phones to dodge texting fees, as it more or less accomplishes the same thing. Instant-messaging services are being used more and more to facilitate online customer support. Retail websites like L.L. Bean and Pottery Barn utilize IM technology to "live chat" with shoppers in real time to answers questions and provide support. From Google's Gchat to Skype, iChat, and even Facebook, the instant message is used all over the web to connect all kinds of people.

- Be careful not to abuse this tool. Don't repeatedly IM people who do not respond to you.

- IMing can be intrusive in the workplace, so refrain from social chatting during work hours.

- Depending on the site you use, there may or may not be an official recoverable record of IM chats, and those who use it for any business purposes should be aware of this.

VIDEO CHAT

While the idea of the video chat isn't new, a video chat you have from the palm of your hand while on the go is. You don't have to prearrange a FaceTime call, but don't be offended if some people ignore a FaceTime call and call you back with just audio. For any video call, be it from a smartphone, tablet, laptop, or desktop computer, you'll make it easier for the person you're talking to if you:

- Check—and understand—your technology in advance. If the person you want to video chat with isn't familiar with how to do it, offer to walk them through the steps.

- Have a phone number as backup if you're using programs like iChat or GoToMeeting.

- Dress as you would if you were meeting up in person (this goes double for work video calls!).

- Keep eye contact as close to the camera as you can.

- Think about the backdrop your caller will see (again, this goes double for work video calls!).

BROWSING AND GAMES

Though Internet browsing and playing games are two different things, their effect on the people around you is more or less the same. As a fun distraction in a waiting area or when on your own, they're great. But when you are with other people who deserve your attention, resist the urge to play, and put the device away until later. When you're in public, mute the device or use headphones when watching videos or playing games that have audio.

A CAPTIVE AUDIENCE

If a tree falls in the woods and no one is there to hear it, does it make any noise? If I'm walking down a city street, talking to a friend on the phone, and I'm not getting in anyone's way or causing a traffic accident because I'm distracted, is it rude? Nope. Mobile devices are beloved for their fancy-pants features, but they're also loved for being exactly that—mobile. We've talked about the idea that it matters how our actions affect others. When those others—especially strangers who don't care about cutting us slack or understanding our reasons—have no choice but to listen to our conversation (or music or movie or game), they have every right to give us a dirty look. It's the captive audience we have to watch out for when we're in public. Here are some places where you might want to be extra-thoughtful about how you use a mobile device.

OUT AND ABOUT

Elevators. Theaters. Restaurants. Waiting areas. Lines. Sporting events. Gyms. Public restrooms. Coffee shops. These are some of the most likely spots a captive audience might be found—and thus are the least conducive to carrying on a phone conversation or listening to audio without headphones. (We'll look at travel situations later.)

Whenever possible, ignore a call or step outside when you are in one of these places. If you really have to answer, keep it quiet and short, and consider apologizing to the people around you. Nothing makes waiting at a crowded gate for a delayed flight worse than having to listen to a twenty-five-minute, one-sided conversation about whether the caller should get a second cat (true story).

Now imagine sitting on a park bench on a sunny day, enjoying lunch and a phone call to a friend you haven't talked to in ages. Anyone joining you understands the situation they are inserting themselves into. But to be on the phone and join someone already sitting on a park bench just isn't cool.

What's the Big Deal?

Have you ever wondered why it's so hard to not listen to someone's cell-phone conversation? If two people were sitting next to you having a conversation, you could tune them out and read your book or newspaper, no problem. But if a person next to you starts a cell-phone call, you can't help but listen to and complain (at least to yourself) about the lout who subjected you to his conversation. It's simple, really. When you hear both sides of a conversation, it's complete. But when you hear only one side of the conversation, you instinctively start wondering how the other person is responding and, in your head, you become part of that conversation.

WIRELESS AWARENESS IN PUBLIC

At the Emily Post Institute, one of the biggest complaints I hear about mobile devices is how the people who use them appear to be lost in their own worlds. My favorite examples are those of New Yorkers who get so frustrated at the slow, distracted, and lackadaisical way in which people using a smartphone or tablet clog up the streets or, more specifically, the subway entrances.

While taking your time might be a virtue in the small town I grew up in, New York street culture requires that you get moving, keep up, or get out of the way. It is important to stay aware of your surroundings when using a mobile device in a place like that. It is especially true anywhere you could physically be in someone's way. In busy terminals, subway and store entrances, crosswalks, stairways, and escalators, beware and be aware that you are not in the way of those moving around you when using your mobile device.

DON'T CHECK OUT ON YOUR CHECKOUT PERSON

Of all the captive audiences, there is one that gets a particularly raw deal. Listening to someone chat on their phone while in the grocery line is annoying—got it. If that wasn't annoying enough, it becomes cringe-worthy when that person carries on chatting while ignoring the checkout person. Inevitably, they'll need to answer a question. "Wait, wait, Charlie, hang on. Hang on. I'm checking out. Hold on, I'll be right back." And then to the checkout clerk, "OK, sorry, what did you say?" As in, "I'm ready to pay attention now that I've wasted everyone else's time." It's rude to just ignore someone who is helping you. Yes, it's their job. And it's yours to be nice and pay attention.

PLANES, TRAINS, AND AUTOMOBILES

Buses, subways, and trains have all had their fair share of controversial moments with digital devices. A friend told me a story about a woman whose volume on her iPod was up so loud that everyone else on a packed subway car was subjected to her music. To show her just how loud, the person sitting next to her starting belting along to the song. Commuters in specially designated quiet cars are also not shy about chastising rule-breakers. But somehow air travel seems to bring out the worst in some people. It certainly brought out the worst in Alec Baldwin when he refused to stop playing Words with Friends (a Scrabble-like phone app whose players can easily become obsessed with it) and wouldn't turn off his mobile phone after the flight attendants had closed the airplane's doors. The contretemps escalated and resulted in Baldwin being thrown off the plane. While rare, it illustrates the stubborn entitlement some people feel when it comes to using their digital devices whenever they want.

PLANES

Flying is an unusual form of public transportation. There are governmental safety rules and regulations to follow. You're sold a specific seat and are required to sit in it with little or no option to move should you have a seatmate who smells, snores, talks on his phone, or watches what you consider to be inappropriate material on his computer. If there happens to be an empty seat nearby, you can try switching, but there is often no escape at ten thousand feet. Airplanes are more crowded than ever before, and many of the niceties from the bygone era of flying are truly bye and gone. Now wireless service in flight is upon us (and yes, horror stories of people using it to make Skype phone calls have begun). Full-on cell phone service is rumored to be coming to the friendly skies—and trust me, they won't stay so friendly.

PREFLIGHT

Whether it is locating the nearest coffee shop, checking flight status on an app, reading last-minute itinerary changes via e-mail, or flashing your digital boarding pass, mobile devices are now key components of air travel. And mobile etiquette for air travel begins before you even leave the ground:

- In the TSA line, it's simple: the rules say "no cell-phone use." So put it away.

- Speaking of the TSA line, be ready to place your laptop or iPad in a separate bin for scanning. Don't have them so buried in your carry-on luggage that you have to pack and unpack every item every time you go through security.

- Always bring your own headphones if you plan to listen to any music, videos, movies, or sound-enhanced games. They will likely be better quality than what you are given or can purchase on board.

- Don't hog the limited power outlets in the terminal. If you need to plug in to power up, be sure that when you set up camp you are not in the way of anyone either trying to reach the adjacent outlet or simply trying to get by. Once powered up, unplug and let someone else have a chance.

- Once on board, power off devices when instructed to, and do it in a timely manner (ahem, Alec).

IN THE AIR

If you do use your mobile devices while in flight, be considerate of the people sitting next to you and near you. It's likely you are foisting your technology—and your conversations—on them.

- If you will need your devices try to keep them, and all the accessories you need, with you to avoid having to retrieve them from the overhead bins midflight.

- Always use earbuds or headphones when listening to music or watching a video on your device.

- Take care with the content of the videos you watch. Your neighbors can't help but see what you are watching. Privacy screens help, but don't assume that just because you are using one, it guarantees the person next to or behind you won't see what is on your screen. (See box.)

- Don't snoop. Show your seatmate some respect. Sure you could read everything on their screen, but instead of looking, concentrate on your own book, your own screen, or the view outside and give them some privacy.

- The seat back on today's planes can be a laptop computer's worst enemy. If you plan to recline your seat, take pity on the person behind you and do it slowly. Even better, only recline partway if they are eating or working.

- When you're given the OK to use your phone after landing, keep the inevitable "We've just landed!" calls short. Better yet, consider texting that message.

For Your Eyes Only

On a recent flight, I was watching the innocently titled *Mysteries of Pittsburgh* when I was surprised by a nude love scene. I love the movie, but whoops! I turned it off before I even had a chance to check and see who else might be peering. Better safe than sorry.

It is easy to be lulled into your own world and forget about the people around you. The action movie you think is great could be both wildly inappropriate and

---

completely engrossing for the nine-year-old sitting next to you on the plane or in the gate waiting area. Privacy screens do help (blocking out the view from your sides), but you never know who could be peering over your shoulder. Whether it's a movie or your company's financial spreadsheets, be aware of the content on your screen and of who else might be watching.

TRAINS AND BUSES

These are public places, hence the word "public" in public transportation. Don't assume that other people don't, won't, or can't hear or see what you are saying, watching, or doing on your mobile device. They can, and they will, just like on airplanes.

- Skip calls in favor of texting, and set your text alert to silent or vibrate.

- Always use headphones to listen to audio.

- Keep any content you view appropriate to a public setting.

- When in the quiet car, always follow the posted rules. (See below.)

THE QUIET CAR

Quiet cars and no-cell areas in places like airline club lounges and waiting areas are great. You can elect not to use your device and enjoy the freedom not only from it but also from having to hear others using their devices.

Usually, people follow the rules. But one day I was on an Amtrak train from New York City to Washington, DC. The conductor was coming through the car and passed me. I couldn't help but notice a woman enter the car and stop him. It turned out she was seated in the quiet car. She was frustrated because a couple of people were ignoring the rules and she asked him to do something about it.

Bravo for her. First, she was protecting her rights as a passenger in the quiet car to be free from cell-phone intrusion. Second, rather than complain to the perpetrators herself, she took her complaint to a person in charge and had him deal with it. And he did.

APPROACHING STRANGERS

It's nice to talk about respecting your fellow travelers, but what if they don't respect you? This is a question of picking your battles. While some strangers react well to a simple "Would you mind turning down the volume? Thanks," others will blatantly disregard your request, or worse, turn up the volume, just to be contrary. You might also get into an argument. Whenever possible, raise your concern with someone who has the standing to address the issue. A word from a manager, usher, flight attendant, conductor, or driver can be just the ticket, as they have the authority to take action if the behavior doesn't change. Consider changing your seat if that will easily remove you from the problem, and if you do choose to engage a stranger, be sure to ask nicely no matter how annoyed you are. That means a "please" and a preemptive "thanks," a smile, and no gritted teeth. The old adage about flies and honey is true, but it's not just about getting what you want. It's about acting with grace and poise no matter what you're faced with. That, after all, is the true test of good manners.

3

SOCIAL NETWORKING

As the Internet has become part of the fabric of our lives, social networks are connecting more people in more ways than most people imagined was possible even a few years ago. Yet, no matter what social network connects us, it is unlikely that the number of people with whom we are capable of maintaining a meaningful connection will increase dramatically. While the potential for new communication mediums to increase the size of our social pool exists, I agree with one prominent anthropologist that the ceiling on manageable relationships is around 150 people. Now, you may read this and think, What? I have more than 400 Facebook friends. I'm connected to 350 professionals on LinkedIn. There are more than 200 contacts in my iPhone. What is he talking about?

Allow me to introduce you to Robin Ian MacDonald Dunbar, a British anthropologist and evolutionary psychologist, currently a professor at the University of Oxford. He is best known for formulating Dunbar's number, a measurement he described in the journal *Behavioral and Brain Sciences* as the "cognitive limit to the number of individuals with whom any one person can maintain stable relationships," and his research suggests that functional social groups max out at about 150 people.

People seem to have an affinity for groups this size and are able to maintain effective social relationships when operating on this scale. Large organizations, from militaries to corporations, often function best when organized into subgroups of roughly 150. Anyone who has seen the film *Gladiator* knows this isn't a new concept: more than two millennia ago, Roman armies were grouped into legions and then smaller groups of cohorts, numbering approximately 150 men, to operate more efficiently. Today there are so many options for connecting with friends that a network of only 150 people seems comparatively small. After all, Ashton Kutcher had more than eight million Twitter followers at his peak.

I think the sheer number of human contacts that social networks make possible overwhelms people. It's not hard to acquire a seemingly endless supply of relationship threads to keep track of, and those in turn multiply with each new social networking site you join. It's an understandable worry that individual relationships will suffer if your attention is overly divided.

But the important relationships in your life won't go anywhere just because you friend the members of your recreational softball team or reconnect online with everyone from your graduating class after your tenth high school reunion. These connections are fun to rediscover, and it can be nice to keep tabs on people you had lost touch with, but at the end of the day I think Dunbar is right: you'll still probably maintain close friendships with a more select group. A true case of having your cake and eating it too, if ever there was one.

YOUR 150 AND BEYOND

So who are you likely to meet in the world of social networking? Let's take a look.

FRIENDS

These are your current circles of friends, and in some cases acquaintances. Your best friends and wider circle of friends. The friends you kept in touch with from school, summer camp, or past jobs. The friend you made during an eight-hour layover. Your running group, book club, and neighbors. It's the people you have a phone number for, as well as the ones you run into on a regular basis even if you wouldn't call them up to go for a coffee.

What Is a Facebook "Friend"?

The practice of labeling contacts on Facebook as "friends" has led to a redefinition of the term. I have received many "friend" requests from people I barely know or have never even heard of. Perhaps we had a mutual friend or a mutual interest. Is that really sufficient for a relationship defined as friendship? I've also gotten friend requests from people I work with but don't socialize with. Exactly what type of relationship does the word "friend" really describe? I have one friend—a real-world one—who has switched from Facebook to Google+ in large part because all contacts are *not* called friends. He was simply never comfortable with the way Facebook labeled all his contacts "friends."

(For more on the definition of Facebook friends, see "Facebook Translated" in chapter 4, Facebook, pages 54–55.)

FAMILY

Most of us don't usually socialize with our friends and family at the same time, yet Facebook alone potentially puts us in a situation to do exactly that. Parents, kids, siblings, aunts, uncles, cousins, grandparents—social-networking sites can be great for keeping far-flung families connected. They can also help give structure and boundaries to more difficult relationships. As long as your family is even partially functional, it's generally worth it to accept friend and connection requests from family members. There's always the option to limit their access to your account using privacy settings. The alternative is to box them out completely, and then you know what you'll be hearing about at Thanksgiving.

(For more on families and social networks, see chapter 9, Family Life.)

BLASTS FROM THE PAST

It used to be that when two people parted ways the old cliché "let's keep in touch" was tossed about to smooth the parting. Now people are experiencing the phenomenon of joining a network like Facebook and having past relationships knock on their digital door. Social ties that once would have been lost can now linger and reemerge in online spaces.

It can be a pleasant surprise to join a social network and watch the web of personal associations that you experienced over a lifetime take new shape digitally. This has become a shared experience for many who join a large, established social network such as Facebook or Twitter. Be ready for just about any blast from the past. The group from high school that you toured Europe with can share pictures twenty years later. Your winning color team from camp in upstate New York can relive the glory. Class reunions are easier to plan, and long-lost roommates from college are easier to find. And, for better or worse, old flames can reappear.

When the past comes knocking, don't feel compelled to let everyone in. You don't have to accept every friend request or join every new network or community when you receive an invitation. Weigh each decision and only connect with those people you are comfortable being in contact with. You can simply ignore blast-from-the-past requests that you would rather not accept. (See more on ignoring friend requests in chapter 4, Facebook.)

EXES

An ex should know where he or she stands with you because you have already been clear about it offline. Visit or call to break up or break a date. No matter what the circumstances of the breakup, a tweet or Facebook status update should never serve as a notice of the end of a relationship.

There is no "etiquette" about whether to stay connected or to reconnect with an ex on social networks; what works for some former couples would be a disaster for others. The litmus test? If you find you can't keep your comments to each other positive, or if you notice yourself getting upset by what your ex posts to others, cut the tie. You can always reconnect later when emotions aren't as raw. (For more on dating and breaking up online, see chapter 10, Dating.)

COLLEAGUES

There is no single answer about how best to connect with colleagues online. You may choose to tweet with the folks you met at a recent conference, or reconnect on Facebook with the entire marketing department from your first "real" job. You can encourage colleagues to use business sites such as LinkedIn rather than more social networks, such as Facebook, to keep in touch if you prefer. When you're in an online space where you are connected to business colleagues or potential business contacts, act accordingly. There are tools strictly designed for business uses such as LinkedIn (see "LinkedIn" in chapter 11, The Work World). Just like with friends, former colleagues will reemerge online—are these social connections or business contacts? It's important to put them in the right category.

THE OPT-OUTS

Some of your relationships might not migrate online. Whether their job prohibits them from having a Facebook page, they don't use the Internet often (yes, those people exist), or they just aren't comfortable with or interested in social networks, don't leave them out of the loop. Remember to use other media, such as notes, phone calls, or e-mails, to share jokes, links, photos, videos, and news with them, as well as social plans that develop online.

4

FACEBOOK

With Facebook predicted to surpass one billion global users in 2012, it is currently the ultimate social networking site. Facebook's late-twenties billionaire founder, Mark Zuckerberg, and the Oscar-nominated movie *The Social Network*, about its origins, are the stuff of legend.

The digital world evolves so fast that it is impossible to predict when an industry leader will become passé. From AOL to Myspace to Digg, the Internet is littered with the wreckage of the once-dominant. Remember Friendster? Exactly. Yet Facebook seems to have established itself for the foreseeable future. Joining the ranks of Apple and Google, Facebook is an American brand that has captured the world's imagination. Like its fellow industry giants, it is unique in position, if not concept. But with the aforementioned credentials, its role in the revolutions known as the Arab Spring and a $16 billion IPO under its belt, it's clear that an awful lot of us sure do *like* Facebook.

FACEBOOK FACTS

Founded in 2004 by Harvard student Mark Zuckerberg, Facebook began on a single college campus and soon spread to other colleges, to high schools, and eventually to a much broader adult population as well.

Open to anyone over the age of thirteen, Facebook allows users to build personal profiles (also called pages). Profiles may include text, pictures, videos, and links about the user or their interests. Each user is also assigned a wall, which is a virtual bulletin board attached to the profile, where the user or their friends can place more links, pictures, text (called status updates), and video in a running flow.

Facebook works by allowing users to connect a personal profile to other friends, which lets those friends see information about one another and to post information on one another's walls. Each user decides how much access to give to different groups from the general public to friends, a group of friends, or even friends of friends. Users can also customize which kinds of posts different users can see on their profile and wall. Maintaining control over friends and friend groups and giving permission about what information is shared with which friends is how users manage their Facebook accounts.

Each user also gets a home feed that is a personalized glimpse into new posts or changes that friends have made to their walls or profiles. This shows as a flowing real-time virtual bulletin board, similar to a page but including posts from friends (as opposed to just the user's information).

Facebook is also the world's largest online photo-sharing resource. In many ways it has become the world's largest photo album. With its photo-tagging feature, an individual can be identified in a photograph and the photo then links to (and appears on) that person's profile.

Facebook is also famous for its apps (short for applications). Individuals and businesses can build apps (such as games, quizzes, and birthday alerts) to run on Facebook as well. These apps are often unique to the Facebook environment and provide a type of interaction between companies and individuals that is constantly evolving as marketers figure out more and more creative ways to get users' attention. Companies also set up profiles called fan pages (users "like" them instead of friending them), and run contests, sweepstakes, and promotional giveaways through their fan pages as ways to engage Facebook users. Marketers covet the access they get to a very targeted audience via the information you, the user, have input about yourself. You opt into the system to get the benefit of connecting with people, but the trade-off is that you are offering information about yourself and others. However, this is not Big Brother, and it is not compulsory: this exchange is transparent and on the table for you to consider before you sign up.

YOUR PROFILE

Setting up a Facebook profile is about presentation. It's a bit like getting dressed in the morning. While it is not overly complicated, it is important. The choices you'll make about what to share say something about you and how you want others to see you. Think about what you're comfortable sharing and about who you will likely be sharing it with. Fill in as much or as little as you like about your school(s), work, hobbies, interests, hometown, relationship status, birthday, and even politics or religion, though including a profile picture of some sort is standard. Select a profile picture that you are comfortable showing to the world—the whole world, including friends, work colleagues, potential employers, and family members.

Whatever your choices, it's important that your profile reflect the real you. Integrity and truthfulness are important qualities to maintain online. They are what maintains the trust in the relationships we have both online and off, and trust is especially hard to rebuild if lost. Facts can be checked and untruths can be exposed easily in our increasingly connected world.

The whole process of building a public social-media profile may feel indiscreet to some. Where exactly is the line between sharing and narcissism? Sharing is not always indelicate or self-obsessed. There can be a certain generosity to living an open and engaged life. For example, a friend might see I went to Pomona College and want to connect me with his younger brother who is thinking about applying there. Opening up a bit of yourself to a larger community can open unexpected doors. And really, how big a secret is where you went to school anyway?

PROFILE PRIVACY AND THE CHANGING FACE OF FACEBOOK

The good news is that privacy settings allow you to control who on Facebook will see which parts of your account—once you figure the settings out, that is. Learning how to use the privacy features on Facebook is key to having control over who sees what you do on Facebook, and can be a smart way to maintain the image you want to have online. Facebook has been fairly good about addressing the security concerns of users; in fact, for better or worse, it is constantly updating its privacy features. With Timeline, the whole visual architecture of Facebook has recently changed—again. I won't go into the details of the privacy ramifications of this because change is the one constant in the Facebook world, and it is likely to shift again soon.

In fact, one criticism of Facebook is that even though it has privacy settings, they aren't necessarily simple to use. If privacy settings are important to how you control your online image—and they probably are—you'll have to be on the lookout, as administrative changes to the site can affect or even reset your privacy settings to a new default chosen by Facebook. And this can open doors to your online world that you might wish had stayed shut. (This possibility makes a good case for keeping your profile in a state fit to be seen by anyone at any time.)

GROUPS

Use the "group" feature to place friends into useful subsets. For example, consider making a group that you feel very comfortable with to share all of your pictures, status updates, and comments. Some other groups worth considering:

- **Family.** A great group for sharing family business, such as the date of your son's graduation, updates on grandma's 5k fund-raising walk, and photos of weddings, babies, vacations, and family reunions.

- **Colleagues.** Corralling work colleagues into their own group makes it easy to limit how much of your personal information and photos they have access to. Some appropriate pictures and public information is fine, but skip anything that could get you fired up or even fired. Simply avoid anything that you would be uncomfortable having mentioned at work with this group.

- **Private groups.** Once you get the hang of it, you can use this feature to set up groups for sharing just about anything. A bike trip you just took, a study group from school, or a book club you love could all be great candidates for a private group.

FRIENDING

Friending is how you link your Facebook profile to others. Any user can send a friend request to any other user, unless a member has adjusted his privacy settings to restrict access to his profile. You can accept or ignore friend requests with the push of a button (the Ignore button is now labeled "Not Now," but it's still referred to as ignoring). Friend requests that you send to others will be considered in the same way. So, what are the guidelines for sending a friend request? When is it appropriate, when is it not? Generally speaking, people are not offended to receive a friend request. They may accept it. They may not. Here are a few things to consider as you identify the people most likely to appreciate and accept a friend request:

- Friend people you have some reasonable connection to. This includes current friends and family, old friends, colleagues, even fellow club or organization members. (See also "Your 150," in chapter 3, Social Networking, pages 41–44.)

- Searching through friends of friends can be a great way to find people you may already know but aren't Facebook friends with yet, and it's OK to send them friend requests.

- If you have just met someone in person for the first time and you would like to keep in touch on Facebook, ask if they use Facebook and would like to receive a friend request. Then be sure to either follow up with a request or respect their wishes and refrain.

- Facebook is not a dating site, so don't approach people with romance on your brain if you don't know them yet or haven't already met them in person unless you have a good reason.

- Even though Facebook friending features make it easy to friend your whole e-mail list, this is almost never a good idea, as most contact lists include people whose contact info you might need but aren't at all close to, like your plumber or tax accountant.

- Keep in mind that not all users check Facebook every day, so don't expect an immediate reply to a friend request.

What about accepting or ignoring friend requests that come to you? Don't just fly through blindly accepting or rejecting every friend request that you receive. Have a strategy that will help you decide how to handle friend requests. Maybe you are accepting friend requests only from close friends and family;

maybe just people you know in real life. Some people never friend people from their work worlds, others always do so, to avoid missing an opportunity. Your policy might also just be what your gut tells you (just remember to actually check it!). Any one of these choices is OK. Being thoughtful in your choices takes the angst out of choosing who to accept and who to ignore.

When you first join Facebook, it's really fun to discover the way a network of friends takes shape online. The first wave of contacts available to you may be a pleasant surprise; I know it was for me (see below, "A Blast from the Past"). You may begin to see the architecture of your social life mapped in Facebook connections. High school friends, camp friends, college friends, colleagues from your last job, in-laws, or participants from a sports league may be waiting for you to appear to increase their network by just one more. Don't be surprised if just about anyone from your past pops up out of the Facebook ether.

A BLAST FROM THE PAST

Amanda was my high school girlfriend for almost four years. We promised, as only high school sweethearts can, to stay in touch forever and, that whatever happened, we would attend each other's weddings someday. Well, time went by. Many years later, I was deeply surprised and a bit touched by the wedding invitation I received from Amanda. She sounded well and was ready to settle down with her new sweetheart. I ignored the invitation completely: no reply, no gift, no manners, nothing. Doing nothing made my new girlfriend happy, and I really didn't have the money to go or send a gift anyway. I now know it was one of the biggest etiquette mistakes I have ever made.

Years later, I joined Facebook. I quickly found out that Amanda was connected to nearly every Facebook friend I made. Any friend I had in high school or from my hometown was a friend of hers already. Our networks were deep and overlapping in so many ways that I had to face her if I was going to use this new network.

I agonized for days about the best approach. We had not spoken in many, many years. The last interaction we had was my unforgivable disregard for her gracious wedding invitation. All I could do was send a message apologizing for my immature behavior. She responded with her usual grace and poise, expressing that it was entirely understandable and long forgotten. She was simply glad to hear from me after so long. We are now Facebook friends, and the whole episode reminds me of all the unexpected ways that Facebook can bring people together.

IGNORING AND UNFRIENDING

Even though it sounds rude, it is OK to ignore a friend request. It is also OK to unfriend someone. (No alert is sent to the other person when you do either of these things.) People ignore for all kinds of reasons. You do not need to explain yourself when you ignore someone—in fact, it might only serve to highlight the rejection. Business contacts are one exception: people who receive a friend request from a business contact they would rather connect with on LinkedIn will often send a message saying just that. The key here is that a connection is made—just in a venue more appropriate to the relationship.

Whether or not to explain that you are unfriending someone will depend on how well you know the person, how likely you are to ever see them again, and what happened to lead you to this decision. Consider letting someone know what prompted you to unfriend them when there's an offline relationship at stake. Be it inappropriate content they posted or a problem you have with them in the real world, it's a sign of respect for the established offline relationship you have to be direct about your reasons.

FACEBOOK TRANSLATED

Another aspect of the Facebook world that gives many pause is the redefinition of once-common words when they are used in the context of Facebook. Let's take a look at some Facebook vocabulary:

- **Friend.** A Facebook *friend* is anyone you have accepted a friend request from or who has accepted yours. There are as many different ways to think of a Facebook *friend* as there are to think of a friend in real life. The word does not necessarily imply a depth to the relationship, and can easily include mere acquaintances you've connected to that you wouldn't consider a "friend" offline.

- **Like.** A Facebook *like* is simply an acknowledgment of a piece of content. People will often *like* posts without commenting on them; it's a way to associate yourself with or give a nod of approval to someone's post. When a user *likes* a post on Facebook, it registers on their friend's timeline. By *liking* a company or group's fan page, a user establishes a connection with a page and its posts (similar to friending a user).

- **Not Now or Ignore.** *Ignore* is the original language Facebook used to describe passing up a friend invitation. In real life it can be impolite to *ignore* someone who is reaching out to you. Maybe this is why Facebook changed the option to read Not Now when you ignore a friend request. It is perfectly all right to not accept a friend request, and no notice is sent to the person who sent it alerting them to the rejection. (See also "Ignoring and Unfriending," above.)

WALL POSTS AND NEWS FEED

Your wall represents you. What accrues there comes from your posts, your comments to others, photos you are tagged in, and comments or posts from those who you allow to post there. The news feed is a separate stream of content constantly refreshed and added to from the walls of friends. It is a real-time aggregation of content being fed from all the other users a given user is connected to. Each of these areas of Facebook has its own etiquette.

- Avoid oversharing day-to-day events, such as your baby's fourth hiccup this morning, or overly personal information, such as how your bunion surgery went.

- Be careful about posting inflammatory or risqué content. (Think about the dinner-table rule and exclude anything extreme involving sex, religion, or politics.)

- Keep it positive. A recent Intel survey showed that the top digital sharing behavior that annoyed survey respondents the most was people who constantly complain. You don't have to be Mary Sunshine all the time, but avoid complaints, negativity, and rants. Be careful with sarcasm, too, as it doesn't always translate well online.

- Get to know your news feed. Notice which of your friends use their status updates and in what ways their information moves into the feed. It will help you decide both how you like to interact and how those interactions will appear to others. Expect to see updates here from the fan pages you have liked as well, be they media outlets, TV shows, celebrities, retail stores, sports teams, or individual brands.

- You can always delete something you decide you don't want on your wall, but you can't take back the impression it made while it was visible. When you make a wall post, you have the option of selecting whether it appears on the news feed of your friends or not. Consider using this as a filter if you want to share a piece of news with a select group only.

- Be aware that some people don't want to be tagged in photos ever as a matter of policy. Their wish should be respected.

- Be careful when you tag other people in photos or posts. Nothing embarrassing, inappropriate, revealing, or even unflattering should be tagged publicly.

- There are many new kinds of "chain mail" or spam buzzing around on Facebook—from status posts that are meant to be passed on to quizzes and polls that are meant to be fun or insightful when shared with friends. Most people consider these types of posts distracting and treat them as visual white noise to be scrolled past.

TAG, YOU'RE IT

Opening your Facebook account to see that someone has tagged an unflattering or otherwise unapproved photo of you is annoying. The most you can do to avoid less-than-flattering images being connected to your profile is to regularly check the images you're tagged in, and then untag yourself from the ones you don't like. You can also ask the person who posted it to remove the photo if you feel this is important (untagging will un-link it from your page, but the photo will live on, untagged, on their page otherwise).

Check with others before posting or tagging them in a photo unless you're sure they'll approve. Your very best bet is to ask if it's OK to upload when you actually take the picture—then you'll know for sure. "Great picture—is it OK if I post it on Facebook?"

AVOID THE FACEBOOK SCOOP

Don't scoop other people's news. Think engagements, babies, new jobs, buying a house, moving to a new city or town, or planning a party. This can also mean sad news, such as an illness or death. (See also chapter 13, Tough

Times.) If you're unsure whether a subject is ready for prime time, check with your friend first or wait until they have posted or commented about it.

You can also be proactive about protecting your own big announcements. Before she told friends in real life about the birth of her child, a woman I know took her wall down (a setting in privacy features), hiding it from everyone. She wanted to be sure that she had a chance to tell her close family and friends in person before the word got out on her social-media profile. She also knew that no one was going to be able to contain themselves and that the notes of congratulations would be showing up on her wall fast and furious the second she got the word out. This was a smart way to prevent hurt feelings and protect herself from being overwhelmed during the lag time when she was still reaching people with the big news.

The Social-Media Ask

One of my editors on this book made a great point. She mentioned that she often has great success posting questions to her social network. Whether it is Facebook or Twitter, she often gets ideas and suggestions on everything from good places to eat to how to handle a social problem from an extended friend network by simply asking. People love to help out, so go ahead and ask.

APPS

Customized apps that work inside Facebook continue to roll out almost daily. Some are games, others are polls or quizzes, still others work as e-commerce options for those looking to sell products online. Here are a few things to keep in mind when using these features:

- **Games.** From Farmville to Mafia Wars, there is a game for everyone. They can be a blast, but don't push them on those who don't play. However much fun you may be having, don't invite everyone you know to play. Turn off notifications that send status updates every time you clear a new level; nobody wants to see that dominating their news feed.

- The same goes for **quizzes, polls, and surveys.** People who like these will see them in their news feed when you post your results; they don't need an invitation. Every time I am invited to use an app that I suspect is just benefitting someone else by harvesting my e-mail or asking for my feedback, I get a little less inclined to keep the sender as a friend.

EVENT PLANNING

Facebook can be great for real-life event or meeting planning. A few things to think about:

- If you are using Facebook to plan an event, be sure that everyone you want to attend has or uses a Facebook account.

- Double-check that anyone you really want to attend has actually received the invitation. This is still a nontraditional method of planning and even those who have Facebook accounts don't always check them regularly or feel comfortable participating with group events.

- Limit attendance by selecting a guest list or open it up to the world; just think first about which is best for the event you have in mind. Don't invite every friend on your list to the event, party, or fund-raiser you are promoting. Those who are far away or who clearly won't be interested don't need an invitation. In the long run, this will shorten your reach when extending an invitation they might care about. The last thing you want is a reputation as an invitation spammer.

- Include instructions for the best way to reply if you want RSVPs from participants.

THE CONTINUING IMPORTANCE OF THE RSVP

Whether it is online, over the phone, or by old-fashioned snail mail, the RSVP remains a critically important part of good manners. I know that the online RSVP can seem unimportant. The casual nature of the evite seems to imply a casual attitude about the quality or importance of the RSVP. But it is still the first and best way for a guest to assist the host. The rules for RSVP apply to online invitations too.

- If the answer is no, say so. There is nothing more difficult than a question mark on a guest list. Your no won't hurt any feelings or prevent others from coming. In fact, learning to deliver a no well and with grace is a good life skill to cultivate.

- If the answer is yes, let the host know so they can plan accordingly. Then follow through and show up.

- If the answer is maybe, try to figure out a more certain reply as soon as possible. Let your host know that you are checking availability and follow up once you find out the answer. Don't exercise this option too often. Someone who always offers a conditional reply can seem to be waiting for a better invitation.

Even though the standards for RSVP have not changed, the awareness that many people have of these standards is not the same as it used to be. As we have noted, this is particularly true in the digital environment. If you are planning an event and it is important that you know who is attending, a written or phoned invitation may be a preferable method of delivery.

FACEBOOK IM

The instant-message chat feature or Facebook IM is a very popular tool, but take a hint: If someone doesn't reply, leave them alone. Even if you use this feature with someone once, don't overuse it. If you are always the one initiating a chat, maybe wait until someone responds in kind before you assume that they like the interaction. When you do use the IM feature, use it well by:

- Keeping it quick.

- Saying good-bye to finish.

- Not being offended if you don't get a reply.

If you are someone who never uses this feature, consider turning off your IM availability. If you like to use these features but you aren't always available to chat, switch your status to *not available* to clue in your contacts. You'll avoid clogging your message inbox with unread IMs and you'll avoid annoying those who try to reach you unsuccessfully. Conversely, if your best friend and favorite IM buddy is one of those fortunate enough to be employed, be respectful of his working hours and lay off the IMing the same way you would hold off calling or texting during work.

COMMERCE

Promoting your business on Facebook is not just a good idea, it is almost as important as having a website. Facebook is like a little city full of people online, and you want to be in that marketplace. There are some things to think about, just as you would think before opening a new store in a new town. Most users don't mind some commerce, but would also tell you that their primary purpose on Facebook is social engagement, and anything that distracts from that experience can be viewed as bad manners.

- Be sure your company website and Facebook page link to each other and work in tandem.

- Offer value: content, deals, inside information, coupons, genuine discussion, and responses from the company. This can be a great place to test products and get feedback from the most engaged consumers.

- Don't mislead or misrepresent yourself.

- Don't oversell, overpromote, or forget to engage followers with non-promotional posts. Keeping the primary function of Facebook social is very important.

For more on using Facebook for business purposes, see chapter 11, The Work World.

5

TWITTER

Twitter takes online social interaction to an entirely new level of immediacy. Breaking news? It happens in real time (minus the twenty seconds it takes to type and post 140 characters). Celebrity culture? It takes oversharing to a new level. In many ways Twitter has become the world's news feed. When a top-secret helicopter appeared over Abbottabad in 2011, Twitter had the scoop before anyone else.

It is also a news feed of everyday people sharing their lives with one another. Privacy on Twitter is much more straightforward than on Facebook. Your Twitter account is either locked (people have to request to follow you) or unlocked (everyone from your grandmother to your ex-boyfriend can Google you and find your Twitter profile and feed). Twitter is about following (and possibly getting to know), people you would never meet in real life. When my cousin Anna started following a design blogger she liked, she was floored when she received a personal comment in return for acknowledging the blogger. Her reaction: "I'm on her radar? Cool!"

Increasingly, Twitter is used for business promotion and to share information about topics with people you don't know offline. That brings a whole different set of interactions, and with them expectations about how to behave.

HISTORY

Twitter is a microblogging service run through a website owned and operated by Twitter Inc. Twitter was conceived in March 2006 by Jack Dorsey and launched in July of the same year. There are more than 200 million current users, and distribution is global. Users generate and read messages limited to 140 characters, called tweets, to and from followers and people followed. Users can group posts together by topic through the use of hashtags (words or phrases prefixed with a "#" sign) and by user (through the use of "@" symbol as a prefix for a username). Tweets are easy to share, and private messages can be sent to anyone who follows a user. Twitter has become a part of the professional landscape in journalism today and is currently being archived in the Library of Congress.

ACCOUNT SETUP

Setting up an account on Twitter does not require much information. Be thoughtful about why you are using Twitter, and think carefully about the 140-character self-description that others will see. As always, be honest. If you are using Twitter for business, be serious and tell people what you do. If you are using Twitter for fun with friends and family, it is OK to be a bit irreverent and to have some fun with it.

Whatever your purpose, take a minute to choose a good profile picture. This will accompany your tweets and create an impression about you. Don't leave your image set to the default egg, or people won't think you are serious. Think about what kind of background image you want on your account page. This helps complete the process of building and personalizing your look.

TWEETING

Tweets are very short messages—built out of 140 characters. That's all you get: letters, numbers, symbols, and spaces! It is this limitation on tweet length that really defines Twitter, keeping it simple and direct. Because of this restriction, Twitter users employ a code that you need to know to both decipher the tweets you read as well as to build the tweets you send.

DIRECT MESSAGING

In the world of Twitter, "DM" stands for "direct message"—a private message not seen by the public that is sent using Twitter's direct-message feature. If you want to send a piece of private or personal information to someone over Twitter, using this feature is highly recommended. The recipient might choose to share that information, but the original message is delivered only to them.

Always keep in mind that Twitter's default settings are very public; everyone can see everything. Employ the DM when you want to communicate something privately.

KNOW THE CODE

Twitter shorthand conserves space to maximize the content of your message. Twitter uses common characters and abbreviations to define source, topic, and origin, among other things. To use Twitter, here are the symbols that you need to learn and their meanings in the Twitter universe:

- **@.** Who you are tweeting to. This Twitter account will see the tweet you send. For example: Using @EmilyPostInst in a tweet means that we will see this tweet at the Emily Post Institute.

- **#.** What you are tweeting about. This categorizes your tweet with other tweets containing the same hashtag. For example: Using #etiquette in a tweet means that anyone searching the topic of etiquette will see this tweet in that feed.

- **RT.** Stands for "retweet." This indicates that the tweet began somewhere else and credits that account. For example: using RT @EmilyPostInst indicates that the content of the tweet originated from the Emily Post Institute. You can also retweet entire messages automatically without comment using the retweet function.

- **MT.** Indicates a retweet that has been modified in some way, perhaps to allow for some additional commentary.

- **Via/From.** Indicates that information in a tweet came from a source. This is a way to credit information. For example, using via @EmilyPostInst is a quick way to source information obtained from the Emily Post Institute.

- **Pictures.** You can tweet a picture with or without text, either directly from a phone or through a service such as Twitpic that hosts pictures online specifically for use on Twitter.

- **Shortened URLs (web addresses) linking to online content.** There are services that will redirect links from unique URLs, shortened so that they don't eat up the 140-character limit with a long web address. Bit.ly.com and Ow.ly.com are common URL-shortening services and are handy for keeping tweets under the character limit. For example: http://bit.ly/3Heawl will redirect to http://ArtOfManliness .com/category/dress-grooming (saving you a precious 31 characters).

- **GPS location information from mobile devices.** Many devices will allow you to activate location services that include information at the end of a tweet, detailing the time, place, and even type of device the tweet is sent from. Be very careful using this feature; it can be very revealing. This information appears at the end of the tweet and is distinct from the 140-character limit.

> ### Trending Topics
>
> Trending topics are a favorite feature in the Twitterverse. You will see them at your Twitter home page identified as a series of #topics on the right-side of the page. They indicate the most popular current topics on Twitter and are a great jumping-off point for engaging this world. Think of them as current site-wide favorite conversation topics.

WHAT DO YOU SAY?

One person's news is another person's waste of time. Twitter can be a study in the banal when you tweet what you had for breakfast today, or that your car won't start. At the same time, some tweets scoop twenty-four-hour cable news channels and break the juiciest bits of celebrity gossip.

Tweet about things that are of interest to your circle of friends—whether it's a story about your favorite band or a picture of your new puppy. Remember that Twitter is most often used as a conversation. In this context, it's a two-way street and like any conversation you want to be aware of the others involved in it. For the much smaller subset of Twitter users such as self-promoters, marketers, and established brands who employ the platform as a one-way stream of information, the following concepts simply do not apply in the same way. However they, too, should be aware that the vast majority of users expect a multidirectional flow of information in this medium. Here are some guidelines for Twitter courtesies:

- Twitter is a public exchange, not a private network, so be careful with personal information.

- Don't tweet everything, all the time, for no reason. Too many tweets can become a type of spam.

- Consider DM (direct message) thanking or "@" acknowledging people when they follow, mention, or retweet you. If you don't need to "reply all," then a DM thank-you is the polite way to go. It's more personal for the recipient, and it won't clog anyone else's feed.

- Speaking of "@" acknowledging, it is possible to overuse this feature. Because it inserts your tweet into someone else's feed it can be disruptive if you dominate or spam another account with too many of these acknowledgments.

- Always credit sources or label tweets that you forward with "RT" to indicate they are a retweet.

- Don't barrage people with tweets. Give them time to respond and read others' tweets too.

- Be sure to engage in the back-and-forth of the Twitter conversation.

- If auto-feeding/cross-posting to other websites or social media, make sure that what you are tweeting is appropriate for all of the audiences that will see it. For example, the link sent to your Twitter followers who may enjoy your vacation photo gallery may not be the most appropriate content for LinkedIn.

FOLLOWING

You can follow people, businesses, and organizations that interest you. You can search topics to find sources of interest. For example, search the topic of yoga using "#yoga," and you will see tweets where yoga is mentioned. Some of these will be original tweets, some may contain links to web content and retweets about yoga that might be of interest to someone interested in this subject. Following people who share your interests, and who tweet often about a topic that you care about, is a common way to use Twitter and to get the most out of it.

Consider following people who follow you, especially if you are using Twitter for business or personal promotion. However, watch out for spammers and overtly promotional tweeters. (For more on the business uses of Twitter, see chapter 11, The Work World.)

6
_____

ONLINE COMMUNITIES

Whatever form communities take—social, familial, educational, business, political—they are an important part of our lives. Social media and mobile technology greatly influence how established communities function offline. The influence of online communities can be felt nearly everywhere in today's world. They affect our friends, family, work, and personal life.

Online auction sites conduct billions of dollars in business. Four-year college degrees can be earned online from any corner of the globe where there is a viable Internet connection. Videogame players compete with and against one another, across the world. Powerful political coalitions are built and managed through online forums, blogs, and e-mail lists. Every sport and hobby imaginable has an online forum where like-minded "passionistas" can share stories, statistics, and advice. Once highly insular, online communities have opened their forums to the masses. Along the way, each has developed a particular code of conduct. While it is easy to hide behind a made-up username, appropriate behavior while visiting a virtual community is important and a measure of your character, just as it is in your face-to-face communities in your daily life.

Online communities often have a specific purpose: to share information, ideas, and experiences; to meet socially; to play games; or to interact in a work environment. Even though you might never meet the people you connect with in person, it's important to remember that there's still a real, live person who will react to what you type at the other end of the keyboard.

If you are isolated, either geographically or socially, online communities, like other web destinations, can open up a whole new world of social connections. These are great places to find others who already share a common interest. If you are a naturally shy person, you can use these interactions to build your confidence so that when it applies or is appropriate you can eventually move toward face-to-face interactions with greater ease.

A Look at the Landscape

When first doing the research for this book, I was pleasantly surprised by many of the stories that I heard about Internet communities. They came from people in all walks of life and involved issues from the ridiculous to the sublime. One particularly poignant example involved new mothers of very premature babies. There are forums where mothers of premature babies exchange information and resources. At an isolated and trying time in their lives, women can communicate with others going through, or who have gone through, the same thing. They exchange advice, moral support, and even precious resources like the breast milk that has to be pumped and stored ahead of time for their children. New mothers using the Internet to find one another and organize an exchange of critical resources for their children was not what I expected to find when I started to ask people what surprised them about Internet communities.

But the truth is that even the biggest online communities—the ones everyone knows about, the ones that are globally influential and have a dramatic effect on all of our lives—are fundamentally community sites where the users often determine what information the sites contain and how people use them. Let's take a look at a few "community" sites that might surprise you.

YOUTUBE

The largest video-sharing network in the world has become such a force in popular culture, it is easy to forget that YouTube began and still functions primarily as a peer-to-peer video-sharing network. Users set up free personal accounts to post material and comment on one another's videos. YouTube has achieved a great deal of success by allowing other websites to easily display embedded video hosted at YouTube.

WIKIPEDIA

The world's largest online encyclopedia functions as a managed community where users contribute to and review all content. Wikipedia is both a cultural phenomenon as well as the butt of the pervasive online joke about not believing everything that you read on the Internet. A not-for-profit, open-submission, online encyclopedia, Wikipedia has changed the way research is done. While the open and unpaid peer-review process can take some time to verify the truth of all submissions, Wikipedia has set a new standard for baseline information gathering because of its sheer size and number of contributors.

CRAIGSLIST

The message board that could. Craigslist is a very popular open classifieds bulletin board organized into common categories, mainly for buying and selling both goods and services. Years ago, Craigslist made a choice to not adopt a for-profit model of operation, despite having millions of users conducting many millions of dollars in business on its pages. The choice to continue to function without a multimillion-dollar, or even billion-dollar, capital infusion made Craigslist the darling of Internet users looking for an e-commerce refuge from online commercial and corporate interests.

EBAY

Traded on the NASDAQ, eBay Inc. is an online auction site that hosts billions of dollars in business conducted through user-to-user interactions. This site has expanded to provide money-handling services through PayPal and ticket exchanges through StubHub. eBay has become a profitable global corporation with billions of dollars in revenues by successfully hosting the sales accounts of its users.

REDDIT

Reddit has an incredibly diverse community of users who share and evaluate content from all corners of the web. Divided into topic-based subgroups, called subreddits, Reddit allows users to post content and to "up" or "down" rate the postings of others. Positively reviewed content filters up to the front pages, where a large audience browses. Users with a history of sharing good content earn "Karma" points and increase their community standing. It's a fascinatingly complex message board. Subreddits can become their own worlds, with focuses ranging from charity work and fund-raising to pictures of adorably cute pets and baby animals.

WAYS TO PARTICIPATE

Whatever size or kind of online community you are interacting with there are some behaviors that are universal. Self-awareness of your role in any community is critical in deciding the correct ways to behave. Whenever we interact with others, it is important to know not just how we feel or think but how our actions are going to affect and be perceived by others.

Amy Jo Kim, author of the influential book *Community Building on the Web*, has done seminal research on the ways that people interact with online communities. Kim has identified several "personalities" and stages that describe the different ways people participate in these communities. Because each stage has its own behaviors, it's a great launching point for addressing good manners for online communities. See if you can recognize yourself in any of these descriptions.

THE LURKER

The lurker is someone who visits an online community or site, but doesn't actively participate. It's often how you might behave in the "getting-to-know-you" phase of interacting online. Don't think of it as a bad thing; it's not all that different from walking into a party and checking out the scene. This is the initial phase when you have found a site that you like and you start to both discover what's there and also to observe the ways that others use the site. When you are lurking, be sure to check out information pages such as "About Us" or "FAQ" (Frequently Asked Questions) as well as the ways that others comment and respond.

THE NOVICE

The novice is becoming more interested and invested in an online community, visiting often and preparing to post comments and join the conversation. For example, after reading through all of the comments on a NYTimes.com or HuffingtonPost.com story, you may decide to post your own. Or, after reading and trying several different recipes on AllRecipes.com or Epicurious.com, you may decide to share your grandmother's piecrust recipe or comment on the special ingredient you added to ShellFish32's seafood casserole. You've jumped in the pool!

THE REGULAR

You are an established community member, and those who visit or participate with any regularity know who you are. There is a history of interaction between you and others on the site, whether it is reviews of the last five restaurants you've visited or your thoughts on the appropriate size of government. You are now "part of the club." Those who never get past the lurker or novice phases may not fully appreciate the depth of relationships that can develop between regular participants in an online community. You may not realize it, but by participating as a regular, you help set the community standards simply by modeling the types of (I hope polite) interactions that are the site norm.

THE LEADER

Once you have been a regular for a while or have established a reputation, you may become a community leader. You may lead by simply continuing to demonstrate the behavior that makes you a respected member. You might play a more formal role and help to arbitrate or mediate interactions between others. If you value the community, you might even consider how to best give back and support it. There are administrative roles, comment-moderation duties, even fund-raising that could be necessary to keep a community afloat. Consider offering to help with these. At EtiquetteDaily.com, several committed users have become community moderators, a huge source of support to the webmaster (me!)—and something that's added tremendously to the nuance and feel of the site as well as its value.

THE ELDER

At some point, your participation in a community may dwindle and come to an end or an online community may shut down. This is normal and natural. Like any parting or ending, the process of withdrawing from a community can be difficult as well as bittersweet. If you have made friends, be sure to say good-bye, and to say good-bye well. Resist the overly dramatic and oft-used "good-bye cruel world" departure that tends to burn bridges. You never know when you may want to come back for a visit.

Because content often lives on even after websites die, you may find yourself with an ongoing association with an online community with which you no longer participate. Regardless of how you part, be respectful, and think of handling the separation as you would when leaving an employer. Leaving on good terms will only benefit you over the long term.

MESSAGE BOARDS AND FORUMS

Message boards and online forums once ruled the Internet as the dominant online information exchanges and are still an integral part of many websites today. Some forums even preceded the Internet as we now know it. In the early days of the Internet, the message board became the primary community model because it was so simple.

Message boards work like enormous and somewhat complex bulletin boards. Users suggest or post a "topic" to add to the board or join a "thread" in a topic already established and leave comments or questions related to it. Others respond, and a discussion comes to life. Message boards and forums differ from chat rooms in that user comments and exchanges are stored over time and displayed for others to view and learn from. While not the force they once were, these giants have left their mark and still exert a tremendous influence both online and off. Today's message boards and forums cover a wide-ranging list of topics, including those that specialize in diseases and medical information, technology and software, videogames, sports, and more.

Whether you are facing a scary health diagnosis or just looking for other individuals who share common interests, message boards and forums have the power to bring people together in amazingly unique and intimate ways. From organ donation to vintage vinyl record sales, connections made on message boards can be life-altering. You may not know what to expect when you reach out through the keyboard, but you do know that you are reaching out to other human beings. While you may feel a sense of anonymity, you will need to call upon your thoughtfulness, and you will need to treat others with respect and consideration.

Most boards or forums require a new user to register an account associated with an e-mail address before commenting. A board administrator or team is likely to approve and manage the process. Once you have an account, you can log in and participate. Usually, forums have some common elements and features. Being familiar with them will help you use them better.

- Discussion on a board or forum is organized by topic. Look to see if there is already a current topic related to your interest before starting a new one. Otherwise it is like joining a conversation and asking everyone else to start back at the beginning.

- Conversation that develops through back-and-forth comments on a topic is called a "thread." Stick to the topic at hand and reply to those who respond to you.

- Don't ask questions and then disappear. This is a common courtesy, and yet people forget. Check back periodically to see if anyone has replied to you. Thank those who offer help.

- Many sites have features that allow readers to manage what they see. You might be able to turn off comments from a certain user or group of users that you don't like to sift through or even like to read. You can ask to see hidden or unworthy comments to get an idea of how moderators are shaping the discussion and when they are leaving the trash out of view.

- Check the FAQ for community features, such as being able to flag or highlight favorite content so that you can customize and improve your own experience on a site.

The courtesies for online forums are a reflection of how well they work. Since there is no guarantee that anyone will respond to a topic suggestion or comment, it is important to suggest or ask in a way that encourages response. The only way discussions continue is if those involved are interested and engaged. So be nice and play by the rules or risk being ignored.

BLOGGING

Blogs, short for web logs, are simple websites that many people use like an online journal. For many, writing on a blog or reading a blog is a regular activity, like checking the newspaper or jotting in a diary. Blog content is often themed or organized by topic or interest.

Blogs usually allow readers to comment, creating a dialogue. The availability of free blogging platforms (the most popular include WordPress, TypePad, and Blogspot) has made this form of communication available to almost anyone with a bit of computer knowledge or a willingness to learn. The amount of time people spend sharing ideas and experiences on these platforms, both by posting content and in discussions in comments, is staggering.

Nearly every demographic, from mommies and marketers to fashionistas and politicians has woken to the exhilarating power and reach of blogs. They can shape popular opinion and affect media narratives. Regular bloggers experience bonds of affection with readers, a level of familiarity with commentors, and followings that can number in the millions. Regular commenters can get to know one another well, and the user communities that coalesce around certain blogs are vigorous and dynamic.

Just as with online forums and message boards, most blogs share features such as a home page, posts, comments, registered users, and categories. Again, even in these informal settings, appropriate behavior and common courtesy is required. Don't be afraid to jump in and join the discussion by posting comments. This is the beating heart of many blogs and what separates them from a traditional print newspaper or static website. I know people who blog regularly on political sites, image sites, diet sites, biking sites, dance sites, parenting sites, and etiquette sites. You name it, and there is likely a blog about it.

The blogging revolution is now entering a new stage of evolution and growth. Twitter, for example, is often referred to as a microblog. Special-feature blogs like the incredibly popular Tumblr and Pinterest come already set up with built-in social-network integration and have made blogging available, easy, and fun to a whole new audience of social-media and mobile users. (For more on these, see pages 95–97.)

What Would Emily Post Think?

Emily herself was a social animal. She enjoyed the company of friends and contemporaries, an asset that most likely helped make her a keen articulator of common social norms. Before she began or even anticipated her career as a manners writer, Emily embarked on a cross-country road trip in 1915. She wrote about it in a series of articles sent back to New York and published in *Colliers* magazine, and later published as *By Motor to the Golden Gate*. (Sounds like the 1915 version of a blog, doesn't it?)

At a time when many never ventured more than one hundred miles from home in a lifetime, Emily reveled in her encounters with new people who lived in different ways and in different situations. The original arbiter of American manners greatly enjoyed getting to know the whole of a country that she would help to unite with a common code of behavior. Her cross-country road trip was in many ways an adventure into the growing sense of a national community that she would further help to define.

COMMENTING ONLINE

Just as there are certain rules of etiquette for all polite conversation and social interactions, there are also considerations for how to interact politely online, whether those interactions are taking place on a forum, blog, website, Facebook, or Twitter.

Often, in order to post comments, you are required to become a registered user on a site. This may mean creating a screen name and/or providing an e-mail address. Think about how you want to identify yourself when you register, especially if using your real name and e-mail address, because you are publicly viewable. You are also likely to find that Google may show comments you have made when you search the Internet using your name or e-mail.

You may not be as anonymous as you think. As a webmaster, I am surprised by how often I am asked to remove someone's real—not screen—name from a blog comment (*it can be done*). Inadvertently signing your real name or providing your e-mail address isn't the only way to reveal your identity. There are many ways to be identified online. Personal information or a unique perspective could identify you to those "in the know" as quickly as if you had included your full name and e-mail address.

Consider what you post on the Internet to be public and permanent and think before you fire off any negative product reviews or a passionate political screed. After all, Twitter has already been submitted for permanent archiving in the Library of Congress, so consider the historical implications of what you are about to share!

SEVEN TIPS FOR ONLINE COMMENTERS

1. Stick to the topic at hand.

2. Keep it civil, even if you are feeling passionate.

3. Visit more than once to get a feel for a site and eventually to build a reputation.

4. Notice the tone and nature of the comments that regular or repeat users employ. Are they talking to one another or to a post author? Are they offering opinions, arguing, brainstorming, telling funny stories, posting pictures of pets? Every blog is different.

5. If you write something to another person, stick around or check back frequently to read the reply and respond if appropriate.

6. Be aware of the larger audience that may be reading what you write; it may be seen by many more people than just the person you are responding to.

7. Don't just jump in to try to drum up support for your idea, blog, or website.

General Conversation Guidelines

Tier One: Safe Territory—sports, weather, local celebrities

Tier Two: Approach with Care—religion, politics, sex

Tier Three: Wait Until Invited—personal life, family relations, finances

AVOID THE FLAME WAR

Do the other members of the community a favor: argue well and leave the flame-thrower at home. Nobody wants to read the same old argument, especially with the same people holding the same positions. Certain topics are famous for leading people into notoriously hard-to-resolve positions and, ultimately, to personal attacks. Whether it is as serious as the Israeli-Palestinian conflict or as dated and irrelevant as Sega versus Nintendo, you are not likely to change any minds by ratcheting up the volume or vitriol. When an argument spirals into repetitive and functionally useless territory, it is called a flame war because total destruction is all that is left afterward.

We are never going to agree with everybody. This is true online as well as off. Know your own hot buttons. Don't get drawn into the same arguments, especially with the same people. The heat of the debate may be fuel to your fire, but to everyone else who has to watch, it is simply juvenile.

When an online discussion gets heated:

- Don't make a personal attack on the person you are arguing with.

- Never insult or question someone's intelligence or integrity.

- Address the substance of the argument.

- Stay focused on the topic of the discussion and pay attention to what you are writing to keep your emotions in check.

- Give yourself a moment to cool down before you post a comment or hit Send on an angry e-mail.

- Remind yourself that everything online is both public and permanent. Are you saying something you may regret later?

The Difference Between Fact and Opinion

Opinions are simply people's perspectives. While they may have value, they are neither true nor false. Facts are unambiguous and can be verified. Be sure that any information you rely on or repeat is factually correct to avoid spreading rumors or falsehoods that you've picked up online.

Godwin's Law

"Godwin's Law," created by Mike Godwin in 1990, states: "As an online discussion grows longer, the probability of a comparison involving Nazis or Hitler approaches one." Noted by *The Telegraph* of London as "the most famous of all Internet laws," this theory has a stated corollary: when a person makes a Hitler or Nazi comparison as part of an online argument, they forfeit that argument. In addition to being an observation, Godwin's Law can also be applied: if a commenter mentions Nazis in a discussion thread, the law can be invoked, and they instantly lose the argument.

The tendency for online discussions to devolve into wild exaggerations or insult-laced flame wars is very real. So real, in fact, that it spawned this "law" that mocks the hyperbolic heights where accusations of Hitler-like evil are common to the point of banality. It is also generally a good reminder that hyperbole only serves to discredit.

No Sock Puppets

Users who operate dishonestly face potential banishment. "Sock puppet" user accounts are a classic example, where the same person runs multiple fake users.

The intent is to create the appearance of actual discussion or debate between different people when there is none. When it is so easy to create a user account, the temptation to stage a conversation or debate is simply too much for some dishonest people to resist. This is obviously improper and is almost always a bannable offense.

REPEAT POSTING

Television programmers know that the average attention span of someone with a remote in their hand is something like three seconds. With a mouse it is even less. Sometimes it takes longer for a comment to appear after it has been submitted than this two-second window of attention allows. You may not see the comment you just submitted to a forum for a few minutes after you post. Be patient; it will get there. Repeat postings are a common, overexcited novice mistake and result in the same comment appearing multiple times. It is cute the first few times it happens to a newbie but can become a forum nuisance if it keeps happening or if the same comment is posted fifty times.

Don't Feed the Trolls

People who spend time online trying to be disruptive are called trolls. Don't be a troll. Just because you are not face-to-face with your interlocutor, this does not mean that the people reading what you say don't have feelings or that their time is not valuable and to be respected. Everyone deserves to be treated with respect.

Sometimes trolls are insulting or mean; sometimes they are simply disruptive, which can be almost as annoying. Most blogging software and blogging communities have ways of dealing with or removing trolls and trollish comments, but they are out there and sometimes they get in.

The best policy for dealing with troll behavior is to ignore it. Trolls are usually looking for some kind of reaction or attention and are less likely to continue the behavior the less response they get. Send them back under the bridge they came from. Help the community—don't feed the trolls.

REVIEWS, RECOMMENDATIONS, AND ENDORSEMENTS

Have you ever written a review online? Movies, books, recipes, restaurants, plumbers, hotels, electronics—the products and services to review are seemingly endless. One of the most powerful tools the Internet has to offer is the online review. We love to read online reviews before spending time or money on something. This is one example of how the online community "pays it forward," by sharing its experience and knowledge.

Take care to write reviews that offer a complete picture—the positive as well as the negative. Watch for spelling and grammatical errors that might take away from your message.

Whatever the venue, if you are asked for a recommendation for a person, product, or service and you are not comfortable giving it, say so. You should never feel pressured to vouch for someone or something. This is true for a business recommendation on LinkedIn or for a product review or any other testimonial on a social media site. It is acceptable to say, "John, I'm sorry I'm not able to provide a recommendation for you. Since we didn't work in the same department, I don't think a recommendation from me would help much. Why don't you ask Lars?" If you have a valid reason, provide it in a straightforward manner. If you don't feel comfortable sharing your motivation, simply say, "I'm sorry, I don't think I'm the right person."

DISCLOSURE

Marketers and PR professionals are finding new ways every day to put social-media tools to functional use for business. There are more and more professional expectations around employees' use of these systems, and it is important to know which of these rules and policies apply to you. Regardless of your personal or company policies, there is a very clear expectation that when you post online content related to business or personal profit that disclosure of your role is a critical part of maintaining honest communication. For example, if you work for a company and are commenting on that company's blog or are suggesting a way to use one of its products in a public forum, it is important that you identify yourself as being employed by that company. Or if you are a blogger being paid to promote a product, you should say so. (For more on professional expectations online, see chapter 11, The Work World.)

"But I Read It on the Internet. . . ."

As you spend more time online, it is important to come up with strategies for evaluating the validity of information. Online communities can be great sources of information, but there is some skill to sifting through virtual information. You don't want to continue to spread false or inaccurate information by mistake. Then it is your reputation on the line.

Ask yourself:

- Can I trust the reputation of this source in regard to the facts?

- Am I using an established site with an established record or hard-won position in the industry that they have a clear interest in protecting?

- Can I find a second credible source to verify the information?

- Am I on the website of a print newspaper with a long and established history?

- Is it probable that there is an ombudsman on staff who is professionally responsible for the veracity of what is posted?

"Yes" answers are a strong indicator that the information is legitimate. Some websites have stellar editors and solid reputations; others are simply sounding boards for people to promote whatever they feel like or to post whatever they find amusing. If you are not familiar with the reputation of your source, do a bit of research and verify with other sources to determine how much credence to give it.

What's in a Meme?

"Meme" is a term for an independent unit of information and is related to the concept of "gene." The term was coined by Richard Dawkins and illustrates that information can have a life and evolution of its own. Genes are units of information in biological chemistry. Memes are units of information in human culture and in the human mind. A meme is a piece of information that is passed from person to person. It can be a word, a concept, or even something cultural like a dance.

In order to pass from one person to another, a meme has to be reproduced. This process might change the meme or leave it the same. The reproduction and potential mutation of a meme as it is passed from person to person makes it easy to think of it like a gene. Ideas or memes that are easy to reproduce can spread fast in online communities, but that does not necessarily mean they are true. Try the website KnowYourMeme.com to suss out current trending memes. (For more examples of memes, search YouTube for "Charlie Bit My Finger"; Google "Flying Spaghetti Monster"; or visit the website IcanHasCheezburger.com.)

POLITICS ONLINE

From MoveOn.org to Redstate.com to the DailyKos.com, the Internet has changed the way people engage in the democratic process. Online organizing has changed the nature of politics and, almost as importantly, political fund-raising.

By 2008, the Obama campaign, as well as others, effectively used social media to appeal to millions of small-dollar contributors. Instead of targeting one million-dollar donor, they looked to a million one-dollar donors. Online political organizing has become a high-stakes money game that political insiders take very seriously. Campaigns and organizations that are able to raise funds and publicize successfully online can have a large influence on the political process.

This new layer of communication within the political system is officially here to stay. We may never escape prerecorded robocalls and attack ads, but savvy politicians know that the way to connect with voters today is through the web and social media. The online presence of political candidates, I believe, has led to more social dialogue and offline conversations about candidates and the issues. Because this information is more accessible, the taboo of talking politics has disappeared in many circumstances.

Whether you think the results are good or bad, no one can deny the very important role that political leadership plays in day-to-day life. Taxes, regulations, foreign policy, public schools, and the military all are affected by the day-to-day choices made by elected representatives. With the stakes so high, political discussions and online organizing can be fraught and highly emotional. Keep a cool head and be willing to think twice before posting. (See also "Limiting Life Creep" in chapter 12, When Worlds Collide, page 197.)

THE NEXT WAVE

PINTEREST

Pinterest, a haven for collectors and scrap-bookers, is a social media site that allows members to "pin" images, videos, and other objects to their virtual pin-boards. For example, perhaps you're engaged and want to collect pictures of your favorite wedding dresses from all over the Internet. You can add the "Pin it" tool to your browser's bookmark bar, and use it to copy the images to your pinboard, probably named something like, "Wedding Dresses I Must Have!" You can also endlessly "repin" images from members you follow, either from your dashboard or directly from their Pinterest pinboards.

A few of my colleagues are quite taken with this site. Here are their top tips for successfully navigating the Pinterest community:

- Review other boards to gather ideas before creating your own board.

- Be yourself: use a headshot or graphic that you feel represents what you're all about.

- Put your other social media links on your page if you want people to follow up elsewhere.

- Use creative but clear titles for your pinboards.

- Also, use creative pin titles. (You are required to put some text with each pin—some members just put a "." to use up the space.)

- Credit photos and state sources when pinning. Original sources are always preferable, as they tend to offer something new to the larger community.

- Tag other members with the "@" sign—just like in Twitter.

- If you create images, watermark or put your name/title/identity on the image.

- Know that if you hold your photos and images tightly, Pinterest—and the Internet in general—may not be the place for you to showcase them.

TUMBLR

Tumblr is an easy-to-use blogging platform with an active community of more than 58 million. Founded in 2007, this antecedent to Pinterest continues to grow fast and is designed, like Facebook, to work seamlessly with other social platforms such as Instagram, Spotify, and Polyvore. Tumblr burst onto the scene with a simple and clean graphic interface and user experience that made setting up a high-powered, image-heavy, socially networked blog easy enough for almost anyone to get started.

After a Tumblr-blogger creates their "primary" blog, they can follow other Tumblr blogs, which are broken down by interest areas, such as food, fashion, books, business, design, and photography—the list goes on. These blog posts then show up on your Tumblr blog dashboard, where you can quickly scroll through and click on the posts that interest you. Tumblr is image heavy, and users often share and repost images from other sources along with their own images and text. Like Pinterest, reblogged photos and content link back to the previous source.

Here are a few etiquette tips for engaging in the Tumblr community:

- Tumblr is a very social community, so if you expect followers you need to engage in other Tumblr blogs by following, liking (clicking on the "heart" icon), commenting, and reblogging.

- Crediting sources is always recommended. For example, when you reblog an image, your followers can click on the image to go to the previous source/blog. It is the best practice and most ethical to allow the blog name or URL of the source, which is automatically copied to your Tumblr text box at the top or bottom of your post, to appear. You can comment on, as well as credit, your source in this space as well.

- Asking for followers isn't appropriate. Offer good content and followers will find you.

- Keep it positive. Anonymous accounts whose purpose is to flame or post negative comments drag down the community and hurt the reputation of the service. Some bloggers choose to block all anonymous commenters for this reason.

REPOSTING

The new social blogging platforms like Pinterest and Tumblr make sharing and reposting online content from all kinds of sources incredibly easy. So easy that a whole new wave of attribution etiquette is starting to emerge around them. Crediting sources, while not a historical standard on all sites, is one of the first and most important rules to observe when reblogging content if you intend to participate well on these newer systems. It may take a second to get good at tracking down where something came from when you begin, but it is a great habit to develop for evaluating all kinds of online content and it is the honest thing to do. If you are using these platforms for a business or professional purpose, be extra careful to observe all rules for proper attribution.

KICKSTARTER

According to its website, Kickstarter is "the world's largest funding platform for creative projects." In a nutshell, Kickstarter is like PayPal with a heart and a social-media gloss.

Do you have a project that you are trying to get off the ground? Maybe you're a fashion designer with an eco-friendly line that you want to launch; an eighteen-year-old filmmaker needing support to get to a film festival hosted in China; a game designer with the next World of Warcraft; or a knitter with the newest and best design for producing hammocks for third-world countries. Kickstarter is one venue for raising awareness and funds. Just like with other social-media sites, you have a home page with a unique URL so you can drive people to your site. You can tailor your page with audio, video, and whatever content you feel conveys your message.

The danger with Kickstarter is overdoing it. Since it launched in 2009, Kickstarter has been part of the funding of more than 20,000 creative projects. The appeal, beyond the lure of potential "money for nothing," is that the site is built to make marketing your project easy, appealing, and inexpensive, and that you are part of a community of like-minded entrepreneurs. Like any appeal for money, you want to be careful about whom you ask and how often. Nobody wants to feel like they are being hounded for a donation, and not every altruistic idea that crosses your mind is worthy of a Kickstarter campaign, so don't abuse the system. Striking a balance between a polite request on behalf of a good cause and being a repetitive nuisance is easy to avoid if you remember that your goal is to be an effective fund-raiser, not a spammer. Here are a handful of ways to successfully engage in this crowd-sourcing program:

- Before you even consider posting a project for funding, have all the details and deadlines refined. You should consider yourself accountable for meeting your project goals.

- Your funders are gracious donors and patrons, not cash cows. Be respectful of their generosity.

- Communicate often. If there are any kinks in your process, be honest and clear. Keep conveying your enthusiasm and passion for the project throughout the campaign.

- Thank every single donor who contributed to your project, as personally as you can.

7

GAMING

On my last trip to China I found the northern city of Jilin not dissimilar from my home city of Burlington, Vermont. It wasn't just the way the leaves changed in the fall; several different businesses in a shopping center near the university reminded me of the video arcades of my youth. Row after row of networked computers were lined up in front of big comfy seats and could be rented by the hour to play online games. These game centers were always lively and crowded. I marveled as students from this rural region of northern China swarmed online to play fast-paced action and adventure games with teams of gamers from all over the world. We have come a long way from Pong.

Humans love to play games. How we play with one another is a fundamental social skill, and the way we do it affects the quality of our relationships. Whether it is Modern Warfare 3 or Words with Friends, the world of electronic games touches just about everyone. It's also a big business. The year 2011 saw the biggest releases of videogames in history, and the industry continues to grow. The fact that one of the most lucrative endorsements available to a professional athlete is for a videogame speaks volumes. In fact, Hollywood movie studios build videogames to release concurrently with the latest films because they often make more money than the film.

Besides the millions of gamers playing on their own computers and game machines, global networks of gamers make up some of the biggest, strongest, and most engaged Internet communities on the planet. Given that, let's look at the basics of good sportsmanship, mobile-device gaming, online gaming, and online gambling.

GOOD SPORTSMANSHIP

Never forget the big picture. Even when you are just playing videogames, no matter how you compete, it is important to remember good sportsmanship. Online or off, you are more fun to play with if you keep a good attitude and obey the rules—both written and unwritten—of all competition. Don't be a poor winner or a sore loser. Nobody likes a braggart or a gloater. When you win, acknowledge the play of others, and thank your opponent for the game. When you lose, keep your head up, and congratulate the winner. Sulking, pouting, and complaining are the marks of a sore loser.

The story of Leroy Jenkins is one example of out-of-control game play that falls somewhere between a colossal joke and a cautionary tale. This meme is worth a Google search and illustrates the importance of being in harmony with fellow gamers and meeting unwritten expectations about good game play. Leroy's ill-considered and over-excited move wasted the careful planning of his fellow gamers and, as a result, he will forever live in Internet infamy for his rash decision.

MOBILE GAMES

What was once the territory of nerds and teenagers is now the playground of every adult who ever played with a slingshot or enjoyed Scrabble as a child. The simplicity and ease of play allowed by touch-screen mobile devices that come with built-in game networks and game apps such as Angry Birds and Words with Friends has put the joys of e-gaming into hands all over the world. This new generation of gamers is learning a whole new etiquette for playing games online or on their phones. Here are some things to keep in mind when playing on your mobile device:

- Stay aware of your surroundings. Don't become so engrossed you become a hazard, a bore, or a boor.

- Safety comes first! No gaming while driving. Put both hands on the wheel and wait till you get there, please.

- Pay attention to the people you are with. Just as you wouldn't take a call or send a long text in the middle of a conversation or social outing, don't interrupt what you are doing with others to play your game.

- Don't change the settings on someone else's game, especially those that are obscure or difficult to reset. If you must change the settings, be sure to change them back when you are done.

- If you are playing a game on a device that belongs to someone else, don't beat levels that they have not unlocked yet, unless you have their permission to do so.

- Don't let active games languish. Pay attention to the pace of games played with opponents, and keep play moving by keeping game appointments or proceeding when it is your turn.

- Be careful about playing during work hours—it will be viewed as unprofessional.

- Build your opponent network thoughtfully. New toys are fun, but avoid the temptation to bug everyone you know to play your new game right away.

NETWORK GAMING

From the online high-score center for your favorite mobile phone or Facebook game to the 3-D arcades in London's Piccadilly Circus, the world of online and network gaming is truly its own universe. Vast and diverse, there is almost no way to peek into it without playing your way in. Gaming communities are some of the biggest and longest-established online communities. The culture can be layered and self-referential in nature. Trying to decipher community-specific standards and norms can be an elaborate process, both in terms of how games are played and the history behind them.

The more established a community, the more time it will take to pass successfully through the stages of participation. Here are a couple of things to keep in mind as you break your way in.

- When you decide to join a gaming community, give yourself plenty of time to figure it out.

- Find some other novice users and play with them. Get to know the game and the environment with those who are playing at your level. You won't inconvenience experienced players, and it will be more fun.

- Keep appointments with other gamers.

- If you are more experienced and you can help out a rookie, do. Everyone has to start somewhere, and a lot can be gained by taking a moment to help someone out.

- Take it seriously, but not too seriously. Play hard. Enjoy the competition.

- Don't cheat. Secret passages to higher levels and invincibility codes hidden in your favorite game are one thing, but your Words with Friends competitor might not like to learn you use a cheat site every time you get stuck or need a score boost in a game.

- Keep it in perspective. Competition can bring out the passionate competitor in anyone, so beware of the tendency to get completely sucked into the virtual world. Be sure you are not getting so drawn into games that you are missing out on other social opportunities, and remember to check in with the people you see in person every day.

- Put the game down: at dinner, in theaters, during meetings, or while in bathroom stalls. A good rule of thumb is to leave the game in your pocket anywhere you shouldn't be texting or taking a phone call.

TRASH TALKING

Have you ever been "pwned"—a gamer's way of claiming they "owned" you after serving up a defeat? This meme began with a misspelling in the World of Warcraft game but has spread across the Internet and its sustained popularity illustrates just how ingrained the culture of spirited boasting really is among competitors. Some of the fun of gaming is trash talking your opponent, good-naturedly dissing his move or team, and bragging about your own skill. Be careful not to overdo it and become "that guy" (or girl) who crosses the line into the obnoxious or inflammatory. Be sure to:

- Avoid being negative all the time, either about your skill or luck or your opponent's.

- Know your audience. Language for your virtual war game most likely isn't appropriate for your Words with Friends community.

- Don't overdo it. Know when to stop trash talking and be careful about teasing another player too much about a loss.

A GAMER'S STORY

Chris is the gaming man. We used to play the *Star Wars* game Rebel Commander for endless hours on his dorm-room supercomputer. We would play late into the night while the world went to sleep and then woke up around us. Eventually the demands of organic chemistry ended the fun for me.

Chris went on to bigger and better games. He was an early player of Ever-Quest, an elaborate networked role-playing game (RPG) a lot like Dungeons & Dragons, only with a team of online dungeon masters constantly expanding a digital playing environment. Chris was part of a cutting-edge team of game characters who gathered in this virtual world to take advantage of each player's unique skills and talents. They met online to perform quests in a shared imaginary world full of monsters and magic.

One day when I went to visit him, he was not at his usual game station amid the multiple screens, piled-up pizza boxes, and stacks of Coke cans. He explained that he was writing a letter to his gaming team. He was going to leave for Europe to travel for a year with his girlfriend, and he was planning on selling his character. He was letting his fellow gamers know that despite a two-year commitment to a gaming team, he had to spend some quality time with the woman he hoped to marry someday.

The items that he had acquired in the game held real value to current players. He was able to sell some of these virtual items for actual money and made several thousand dollars to help bankroll the trip he was planning to Europe. His teammates were sorry to lose a great player but were happy to have the chance to buy some virtual gear and wish a friend well in the next stage of his life.

Chris proposed to the woman he loved in the Italian Alps later that summer, and they lived happily ever after.

He went on to study game theory and has worked for gaming companies on and off while raising his kids. There is no one I know more committed to fun and bringing people together for good times. At the same time, at the most important time in his life, he knew to put the keyboard down and invest time in the relationship he had with the real-life person he hoped to share his real-world life with.

"All Your Base Are Belong to Us"

This bad translation from an early version of the Sega game Zero Wing, adapted quickly for release in the United States, is an Internet meme itself. Don't worry if you don't get it—that's the point. Originally it became popular as a friendly way to trash talk among gamers using lingo recognizable only to videogame fans. Now it is just a fun thing to say that shows you were either playing videogames in the days when Sega still had its own game console, or at least know a thing or two about how gamers talk to one another. Or maybe you picked up this meme elsewhere. Gaming culture has had an influence far beyond its own world and this meme has spread far and wide.

ONLINE GAMBLING: WHEN MONEY IS ON THE LINE

Not all games are just fun and games: the nearest casino could be in your living room, or maybe it is in your office or even in your pocket. Please be extra careful when money is on the line! Respect your personal limits: Never risk more than you can afford to lose. Games are no fun when lives are ruined.

Online gambling can feel very similar to playing any other online game, from Scrabble to the latest simulation game, only the stakes are real. Whether it is online poker or a sports book, when you wager money, you are responsible for your bets and can end up in serious trouble if you aren't able to comfortably afford it. Keep these things in mind when betting online:

- Don't get too high when you win. When money is changing hands, it is easy to get emotional. Avoid boasting, bragging, and celebrating in the face of losers.

- Don't get too low when you lose. Avoid ranting, and don't blame others for your loss or accuse them of unfair play.

- Know the rules of the game you are playing. Not every game of poker is run the same way, so even if you are an old hand be sure to check.

- Be careful you are not breaking the law. Just because something is possible, that does not mean it is legal. Find out what the laws are about online gambling wherever you are. They are sure to vary state to state and country to country, so be extra careful when you are traveling.

- You may be responsible for reporting your winnings on your tax return.

- Follow the rules of the game and the unwritten rules of being a good sport. And remember, games are meant to be fun, so enjoy yourself.

People have very different feelings about gambling. What is simple fun for one person might be fundamentally immoral or a cause of great personal tragedy for someone else. Be sure to approach this topic with care however you might bring it up. Don't be too quick to assume that everyone shares your particular perspective on this activity.

8

PHOTO SHARING

Imagine a giant photo album containing pictures of everyone on the planet and you're close to imagining how the Internet is evolving. Without a doubt, photo sharing is one of the most popular online family and friend activities. In 2011 Facebook surpassed Flickr as the largest photo-sharing service on the Internet. Sites supported by smartphone apps that allow users to add cool photo filters, such as Hipstamatic and Instagram (the latter of which is now owned by Facebook), have added to the explosion of digital photos populating the Internet.

Anyone with a smartphone has a built-in camera that takes high-quality pictures. Tag your sister's photo with her name, and a program on your computer could tag all other photos in your picture files that include her with her name as well. Cameras and computers with simple gallery templates plug into flat-screen TVs with ease; for better or worse, the family vacation photo slideshow has a new lease on life. The capability to store and share photos online makes it easier and easier to share them with family, friends, and everyone else. Now that there are so many photos, thinking about what to share, as well as when and how, is increasingly important, both to edit the overwhelming volume, and to make sure the photos we post are appropriate.

RULES FOR PHOTO SHARING

Once a photo is out on the web, it's possible that it's there forever. Make it a point to:

- Respect copyrights.

- Never take a photo without someone's knowledge.

- Always ask the subject's permission before posting a picture. Even then, parents may want kids to check with them before posting any pictures.

- Never post a picture that could be embarrassing to someone, now or in the future. Remember, that photo is now potentially out there forever.

- Never post or tag pictures of other people's children without parental permission (for example at a birthday party), and be sure to use the privacy controls on your social network site to control who can see the pictures you post of your children.

WITH PICTURES EVERYWHERE, WHAT IS TMI?

It used to be that when a new baby arrived, everyone received a card with date of birth, sex, weight, length, and a short note that hopefully reported that everyone is well. Now you often see these stats online, instead. "Is this OK?" you might ask. Of course it is. When my cousin had his first child, we all received the vital stats vie e-mail or snail mail but with an important addition: pictures. They were wonderful pictures of baby, baby and Mom, baby and Dad, and more of baby. So cute! A few photos that show and share the joy are the best. But keep in mind that it can be overdone. Dozens of photos is probably too many. (And pictures of the birth itself are definitely TMI for most audiences!)

Save Your Personal and Family Pictures

When you ask people what they would grab if their house was on fire, many say, "I'd grab my photo albums. They're irreplaceable!" My answer to this question is "laptop and external hard drive" for the same reason. Save and back up your digital photographs and videos in several locations—don't just move them from a camera to a computer. Have safe and recoverable backups of all the images you care about. You can lose all of your most treasured photographed memories with the crash of a single computer or the loss of a single device.

PHOTO TAGGING

Imagine this: You receive a notice on your Facebook page that you have been tagged. You follow the link to check it out. Ouch! There you are, in all of your twenty-one-year-old glory, exploring the bohemian lifestyle with a bunch of friends from college. Your buddies think this is a great walk down memory lane, but you have a job interview tomorrow. . . .

Tagging photos is the process of identifying the people who are present in a picture. Whenever possible, you should ask someone ahead of time if it's OK that you tag them, as it is important to be careful and considerate where you tag photos of people and display them online. While it is true that everyone should be aware of who is taking a picture of them and for what purpose, the reality is that this is not always possible. When you tag an image with someone's name, you are publicly and perhaps permanently exposing that person in some way.

Some groups of friends as well as families like to share photos in public and also private forums so that more people can enjoy them. But before tagging a photo, it is a good idea to ask yourself, "If I were this person, how would I feel having this image in the public domain?" Then use a standard that is even a bit *more* stringent than the one you would apply for yourself. After all, you are making a judgment call on behalf of someone else, so defaulting to a higher level of discretion is a good idea. If someone asks you to untag a picture or take it down, you should do so right away.

On the flip side, if you see a photo of yourself online that you want removed, let the person who posted it know. Something along the lines of "Hi, Sara! The day at the beach was really fun, but would you please take down any of the pictures that I'm in? Thanks!" Remember, untagging only unlinks the photo from being seen on your account; until it is actually taken down, it is still out there, just not connected to you. Site protocols can vary, so get familiar with the technology to be sure the solution you request will be enough.

DON'T TAG . . .

- People in potentially embarrassing situations.

- Children without parental consent.

- People drinking alcohol or smoking.

- People in sexually compromising situations.

- People in a compromising situation with someone other than their significant other or spouse.

SHARING PICTURES WITH FAMILY AND FRIENDS

It used to be that when friends or relatives came over, out would come the family album or the slide projector. Today's digital version displayed on a home theater has just as much potential to thrill or bore, and the audience is just as captive.

So, don't bore them. A friend returned from a trip to Ireland and sent me a link to the photos she had posted of her travels—all 1,246 of them. Multiple photos of every shamrock, castle, pub, and leprechaun. *Zzzz* . . . Do everyone a favor and edit the album before you share it, be it online or when displayed on your TV. Leaving the editing of family and vacation pictures to your audience truly takes laziness to a whole new level.

OLD-SCHOOL ALBUMS 2.0

So you've stored and backed up your thousands of digital photos. You've sent friends links to albums you've posted online. You've even had the bike group over to see the (edited!) pics from the last trip. Now all those pictures rest in peace on your hard drive, rarely to be seen again.

The physical photo album is becoming popular again for just that reason, but, like everything else, it too has had a makeover. No more cutting and pasting or sticky overlays. Online services allow you to create and style your own album, complete with your narrative, then they print and send it to you as a bound book. What a great gift for the other members of your trip, as a record of your baby's first year, or an anniversary gift of all those wedding pictures that would otherwise languish on a disc.

9

FAMILY LIFE

I knew we were living in a brave new world when we celebrated the first Face-Time Christmas with the Post family. Three generations, ranging in age from twenty-two to eighty-nine, were clustered around an iPhone cooing at a fourth-generation toddler spending time with the other side of his family down South. On the phone, when the little fourth-gen toddler saw his granddad peer over his great-granddad's shoulder, he smiled and laughed in recognition. His great-granddad in turn laughed out loud at the obvious joy on the little guy's face. The interactions were all so real and immediate it felt like everyone was in the same room. Watching this, I remarked what a great iPhone commercial this would make.

Mobile devices and the interconnectivity they provide are part of growing up and growing older today. Parents of children as young as eighteen months find themselves losing their phone or tablet to chubby-fingered toddlers adept enough to navigate touch screens and activate apps. Visit any family-style restaurant and you'll see myriad mobile devices entertaining children of all ages while Mom and Dad steal a few minutes of uninterrupted conversation before dinner is served. Tweens await the purchase of their first mobile device with the level of anticipation once reserved for life events such as getting a driver's license, purchasing a car, or having a sweet-sixteen party. Parents have discovered whole new parameters when disciplining their teens. What good is it to say, "You're grounded," when your teen can retreat to a WiFi-enabled bedroom with a smartphone? But take away a teen's Internet access for twenty-four hours and they quickly get the message.

What do toddlers and teenagers have in common? They have not known a world without web access or mobile devices. What does this mean for parents? Mobile manners should be introduced as early as age two, and taught along with other essential etiquette such as table manners, introductions and greetings, and the importance of please and thank-you.

Spouses also benefit from and love their mobile devices. Managing multiple schedules and keeping track of everyone's whereabouts can now be coordinated through smartphones and apps. And a quick text to your honey during the day can make you feel more connected even when life feels hectic.

At the other end of the age spectrum, elders are enjoying just as many benefits from mobile connectivity. From staying in touch with family and friends to enjoying favorite pastimes, the elderly are online in record numbers. It's equally important to talk to elderly family members under your care about appropriate mobile manners and online safety.

DIGITAL HOUSE RULES

Here are three strategies for staying on top of the technology in your home.

1. AIM FOR A HEALTHY DIGITAL DIET

Just as you wouldn't let your kids eat a diet too high in sugar, make sure your family has a balanced digital diet as well. Balance time spent online and texting with face-to-face conversations; videogames with physical sports or family board games; social-network interactions with real get-togethers with friends. It is so important that children learn how to relate to one another and interact in person. Sitting side by side while texting back and forth doesn't count.

2. ESTABLISH DIGITAL TIME-OUTS

Institute a "no device at the dinner table" rule. This is the time for your family to be together, to reconnect face-to-face without distraction or interruption. Other digital no-go zones might be homework time or the bedroom. Each has pros and cons. Middle-of-the-night texts can keep your kids from getting the sleep they need—and some kids won't be able to resist the call of the Pocket Gods in the wee hours. Many kids utilize mobile devices as alarm clocks. If your teen is adamant on keeping his favorite alarm clock, make sure that the LED screen isn't somewhere it can affect his ability to fall asleep, a proven disruption to natural sleep cycles in both teens and adults. However you decide to establish your family's digital time-outs, work together to set reasonable limits and practice observing them—parents, too.

3. Keep Devices in a Public Place, not Bedrooms

You don't have to hang over your kids' shoulders when they are using the computer, but you do want to be able to glance at what they're watching once in a while. Keep family computers in central locations, and have kids use mobile devices such as laptops and smartphones in family areas. That way you can ask your daughter to show you what she's looking at when she laughs out loud. It's probably a funny video, but if it's an offensively funny video, you can have a conversation about why it's not something she should be watching. It's a good idea to check once in a while to see if your teen is regularly clearing his search or download history. That may be a red flag that he is looking at something online that he shouldn't be. Pay attention to other places your child may have online access—school, the public library, friends' houses. Explain that using someone else's computer without asking or without adult supervision is a violation of your trust and that you expect him to abide by your rules wherever he may be.

Be the Parent

The best way to improve the manners of the entire world is to model the behavior that you would like to see in others. This is especially true for parents. Making choices about how to parent in a world of infinite connectivity is serious business. On the one hand it is important to expose children to all of the tools and technology that will become an integral part of their lives; on the other hand it is important to keep them safe as they learn. The ability to navigate online spheres and master mobile-communication technology will be a requirement in education and a baseline expectation for employment for the next generation.

Parents ought to think both about how they provide access and how they monitor their children's use. Sites such as SafeKids.com and ConnectSafely .org offer great advice, guidelines, and discussions for parents wanting to make the Internet experience safe for their kids. Take advantage of parental controls available through operating systems, e-mail accounts, web browsers, friend lists, and mobile-phone accounts to limit and control what your child comes in contact with via computer, tablet, or phone. Don't worry—local libraries, schools, and community centers are excellent resources for learning more about responsible management of your child's online experience. Even the most technophobic parents and guardians can learn what they need to survive the teenage years. Just remember that no online parental control is a substitute for a vigilant, involved parent.

KNOW YOUR TECH

Parents: it behooves you to become proficient with the devices and sites your kids use. That means if you are going to let your children use a smartphone, you need to know how it works and what it's capable of before you put it in their hands. If you are going to provide online access (and I think you're going to hear about it if you don't), as a parent it is up to you to know how your child is going to get access and how you can control it. Tablets, hand-held game devices and MP3 players are all portals to downloadable material. Know what material your kids can access and purchase, and how.

Kids seem to have a faster learning curve on new devices than their parents do, but this is no excuse to throw up your hands. This is not a lost cause. You wouldn't let your six-year-old drive your car, so make a commitment to learning the tech, testing the app, setting limits on downloads, and anything else that you need to do. And if your daughter is way ahead of you, ask her to teach you what she's learned. She can show you how to post a picture on her social network and the two of you can wind up having a valuable shared experience.

PRACTICE WHAT YOU PREACH

You can set all the rules and limits you want as to how your children use their digital devices, but it will do little good if you don't follow them yourself. According to Intel's "2011 State of Mobile Etiquette," 46 percent of kids saw Mom or Dad use a mobile phone during dinner, and 49 percent don't think there's anything wrong with that. How about when you text at a red light (59 percent of kids have seen a parent use a mobile device while driving)? Or spend the evening pinning, tweeting, and texting rather than talking to your spouse or significant other? Or when you brag to a friend about all the movies/books/ music you've downloaded for "free." If you do it, that must mean it's OK for them to do it too, right? Some habits—such as diving through your purse to check every status update—may be hard to break, but keeping in mind that your little audience is watching your every move can help you increase your awareness level.

Kids Call the Shots

NPR did a story about the Brooklyn Free School, where the students make decisions that affect school policy. One decision the students took upon themselves was to institute a "no screens policy" every other week. No screens, I thought to myself. What an awesome concept: no computers, no mobile phones or smartphones, no television, nothing with a screen. Turn it off for a week. Not only did they survive, they didn't go back and overturn the vote. It worked.

If students can vote that kind of change for themselves, why not families? At least, how about a No-Screens Saturday? No one glancing down in their laps to thumb a message to a friend or coworker. No one yakking on a phone. No one glued to the television. Instead, families—moms, dads, brothers, sisters, grandparents, and even friends—actually spending time talking to one another.

Give it a try. No-Screens Meals. No-Screens Tuesday. Whatever works for you. Just No Screens. (Although perhaps not during the playoffs!)

GUIDELINES FOR ONLINE CONVERSATIONS

At the other end of every post, every text, and every e-mail is another real-life person. Sure, they may have a virtual-world screen name, but it's not a robot getting the message. Insist that the same behaviors that are expected for in-person interactions at home apply to virtual interactions online. These basics never change:

- It's not OK to lie or spread gossip or rumors. That's dishonest.

- It's not OK to bully or threaten. That's cowardly and mean.

- It's not OK to rant. That's immature and disrespectful.

As they mature, kids will need to know how to adjust their communication style to respect the person they're communicating with: the text-speak they use with peers may be incomprehensible to their grandmother, and it is important they know the difference. As their network grows to include older and younger peers; family members such as cousins, aunts, and uncles; work colleagues; and coaches and teammates, their online profile has the ability to affect their life. Teens may not understand that an online persona has the potential to reach the eyes of college admissions officers or a prospective employer. Parents must prepare kids for a world where their online presence will be part of how they are perceived.

OVERSHARING

There are certain topics, issues, and situations that may be discussed within a family environment that might not be appropriate to share beyond the immediate family or those involved. Whether it is an engagement, a death, or just something extra-goofy that your brother did, certain things should not be shared online where anyone can see them. Discretion is an integral part of good manners, and teaching discretion begins with a forthright discussion within the family about what should and shouldn't be shared publicly.

- Don't scoop good news; wait for your cousin to announce her own engagement.

- Don't announce bad news, such as a death in the family, until the close family and friends have been informed in person.

- Don't reveal family secrets, even if the story about why your brother was grounded is just *too* good.

- Don't air dirty laundry. No one needs to know about the big fight your parents just had.

REVIEW SAFETY RULES

Whether you are six years old or ninety-six years old, there are certain inescapable truths about the digital world:

- Nothing online is private.

- What is online can last forever.

- In the virtual world, people aren't always who they say they are.

No matter how many parental controls you set, it is still possible that your child may wander onto an off-limits site, meet someone in a chat room or on a social-media site, become a victim of online bullying, or post something online that has unintended social consequences. So, from the beginning, teach and reinforce online safety basics. These rules apply to any device that can connect two or more people.

- **Never give personal information to someone you don't know:** Your name, address, town, school, age, birthday, or any ID number you may have such as a driver's license, school ID, or Social Security number.

- **Never say where you are located now or where you are going.** Teach your kids not to publicly reveal their current location or where they might be going in the future, such as to camp or on a visit to their grandparents' house. This is a particularly easy mistake to make on Facebook.

- **Never agree to meet in person someone you met online.** Instruct your kids to let you know right away if an online "friend" asks to meet. This is the time for you to jump in and take charge of the situation. If you do think it's OK—perhaps it really is another nine-year-old chess whiz—accompany your child and make sure.

- **Never assume a person you meet online is who they say they are.** Insist that kids stay on age-appropriate public forums or chat rooms that you can easily monitor (this means no private e-mail exchanges with anyone they meet online), and check out or ask them to introduce you to the people they meet there.

- **Know which sites your child is a registered user of and know their user ID and password.** This is important information to have as a safety precaution and is not intended as a way to interfere with your child's privacy. It's also very helpful in the event that a password or username is lost or forgotten.

By the time your kids are in middle school it's important to talk to them about cyber-bullying and sexting as well. Cyber-bullying is using a social network site (such as Facebook or Twitter), e-mail, texts, or voice mail to intimidate or malign another person. Sexting is posting or texting sexually explicit material about or to someone. Both forms of harassment are illegal and can have dire consequences for the victim and the perpetrator. It's never cool or OK to contribute to or visit websites or even forward messages that make fun of a classmate or acquaintance. Be sure your kids know that if they experience or are aware of cyber-bullying or sexting, they should let you or another responsible adult know immediately. Schools are creating policies around these topics, and you can check with your school district for more information.

Review these safety guidelines with your kids on a regular basis, even when they are teenagers and think they can handle everything. Tell them it's a good reminder for you, too. And while you're at it, make a point to remind your parents as well. (See also chapter 14, Digital Safety.)

AGES AND STAGES FOR MOBILE DEVICES

TODDLERS: TIARAS OPTIONAL

Toddlers are interested in mobile devices—keeping little hands away from your phone, computer, or tablet will be practically impossible. The good news is that even at this young age there are mobile manners you can introduce and begin to teach your child. It's good practice for both of you for what lies ahead. Below are a few mobile manners specific to toddlerhood, and keep reading for more guidelines that can be adjusted for the developmental stage of each child. A young toddler's mobile interactions and time online should be monitored by parents or caregivers. Keep a watchful eye on total screen time—that is, the cumulative time spent watching television; playing videogames; or using a tablet, computer, or mobile device—even for reading or educational purposes. Studies abound on the potential harmful effects of screen time on developing brains. Check with your pediatrician for current guidelines.

- Practice good telephone manners. Using a mobile telephone is a great opportunity to introduce good phone manners. Toddlers are not too young to start to learn this important, life-long skill. If your child is excited to talk on the phone, call Grandma, an aunt, or another sympathetic individual who won't mind spending ten minutes talking to a toddler. Practice saying "hello" and "good-bye" using an inside voice and listening to the other person. This is also something your toddler can practice on their own through play (with a toy phone).

- Take turns. Explain that grabbing a friend's iPod or game device because it's "my turn" is not OK. Teach siblings to share devices and game controls—easier said than done, but don't give up.

> ### The "Digital Babysitter"
>
> iPads instead of crayons at the restaurant, DVDs instead of games like I Spy in the car, and smartphone apps instead of a book in the waiting area are all fine. Don't feel guilty about allowing your kids these distractions. Just set a time limit, make sure the content is age-appropriate, and participate with them when you can.

SMALL REINFORCEMENTS: 5–8 YEARS OLD

At this stage, kids will continue to show interest in mobile devices—especially game devices. So now's a good time to begin searching out resources for age-appropriate content. From websites and computer games to apps and portable game players, what's available on the market for children is immense. Many schools now incorporate websites into the curriculum. Because these sites are also accessible from a home computer, this provides a good opportunity to begin a dialogue about appropriate websites and good online behaviors—and you can branch out with recommendations from teachers, librarians, and other trusted resources.

This is also the time to practice what you preach and model the mobile manners you hope to instill in your children. Be careful to avoid the most egregious behaviors such as texting and driving or talking on the phone while in a checkout line at the grocery store. You can also occasionally point out others' bad behavior and explain why it is inappropriate. This makes for good "car talk." For example,

"Did you notice how the woman in front of us at the grocery store was talking on the phone when she was paying? That wasn't very polite. Do you know why?" You may be surprised how intuitively kids understand that this is disrespectful.

LAYING A STRONG FOUNDATION: 8–12 YEARS OLD

Because this is the age when kids will first be exposed to many different devices and online destinations, this is a critical time for parents and caregivers to establish guidelines. Just as kids need help learning to make good decisions about when to go to bed, what to eat, and what's appropriate to watch on television, they'll need that same kind of guidance for using mobile devices and consuming media online. Be proactive on this topic. Don't wait to set some ground rules until you find your child downloading apps on your phone or playing games on his iPod or game device before he has even risen from bed. It's not difficult, and when done together is a really positive way to tackle what can easily become an out-of-hand situation. Here are some ideas to get started:

- Establish house digital rules. Each family's will be a bit different, but house digital rules establish age-appropriate expectations for kids— who can use which devices and for how long, where in the house the devices reside, and so on. The most important aspect of house digital rules is that they are clearly communicated and consistently followed.

- Ask permission. Request that kids (especially at this age) ask before taking a device to play with or getting on the computer. That way you know when they're online or using a device to play games.

- Age-appropriate material only. Explain to your son or daughter that websites, games, apps, and music, just like television programs, must be approved by Mom or Dad in advance. Be patient and take the time to look at the websites they'd like to visit, or the game or app they'd like to download.

- Share passwords and e-mail addresses. If your child must have an e-mail address or password to access favorite websites or content, you must have a copy of this information. Another alternative would be to allow your child to use your e-mail address to do these things. Explain to your child that this is a safety precaution as well as a way for you to check to see if the family guidelines are being followed, but that you will respect their privacy as much as possible.

TWEENS, TEENS, AND THEIR FIRST MOBILE PHONE

There are few milestones as exciting to a tween or teen as getting their first mobile phone. Some kids report getting their first mobile as young as age eight or nine, but most kids are twelve or thirteen when they get their first mobile phone, according to the most recent data available in a 2009 survey conducted by the Pew Research Center's Internet & American Life Project. And it seems to be trending younger. Why the range? Some parents succumb to peer pressure or the ease of adding another line; others want that connection to know a child has arrived safely from school to the next destination. Regardless of age, make sure this is a responsibility that your child is ready to handle.

This new rite of passage—the first cell phone—is a uniquely opportune time for parents to instill mobile manners not just in their child, but also within the household. Make these basic manners the standard in your family and they will become clear guidelines for behavior outside the home as well.

MANNERS FOR A CHILD'S FIRST MOBILE PHONE

- Take good care of the phone (don't drop it!). Require your child to use a protective covering and screen for the device and decide in advance who will replace the device if it is lost, broken, or stolen.

- Explain the monthly contract. Mobile phones and the monthly contracts that come with them are expensive and your tween or teen should understand that. Explain the parameters of the mobile phone plan, whether it includes texting and data services, and how to determine if there's an overage that could result in additional fees. Decide in advance how you will handle any problems that arise, and discuss with your child strategies for preventing these things from happening.

- Phone home. Let your children know when they are required to check in with you. Whether it's after school or work, or when they arrive at a friend's house, explain your expectations regarding regular contact.

- Volume and voice. The number-one complaint against cell phone users is loud voices. Speaking loudly forces your conversation on others. Where you are when you take a call matters too. Step away from crowded areas to avoid disturbing others. Also, remind your child that actually saying the words "hello" and "good-bye" are still an important part of good telephone manners.

- When to turn it off or leave it home. Establish when the phone will be left at home or when the ringer will be turned off—each family will have its own list, but possibilities include worship services, restaurants, class, family gatherings, vacation, and the dinner table.

- Follow the school rules. Each school has mobile-phone policies, and following them should be part of your family's house rules. Review the school's policy with your child so that you both understand it and the consequences of failing to comply.

- Talk in appropriate places. When you're with a group of friends, it's OK to take or make a short phone call, but if you're hanging out with one friend don't get on the phone for an extended period of time. Your focus should be on the person you are with.

- Remove earbuds when talking to people. In fact, take out *both* earbuds when talking to anyone else, especially adults.

TEXTING WITH YOUR KIDS

Even though many parents today feel that their kids text more than they speak (and it's perfectly appropriate to establish limits regarding how much texting your child does), remember that texting can also be a boon. Because kids communicate so much via text, they might share things with you in a text that they may have difficultly discussing face-to-face. Getting comfortable texting can help give you access to their world. Don't overlook the value and power of this medium as a vehicle for communicating with your teenager.

KID-FRIENDLY E-MAIL

E-mail can be a great communication tool for children. Kids can correspond with friends and extended family, and e-mail is a great way for kids to stay in touch with grandparents. Look for an e-mail provider that offers appropriate parental controls that allow you to turn on your own filters, manage the address book, and set limits on who can send e-mail to your child. Good options to check out include ZooBah, AOL Kids, and PikLuk. If you're not ready to provide your child with their own e-mail address you can let them use yours.

SOCIAL-NETWORKING SITES

While most social-networking sites do not allow children under age thirteen to maintain their own pages, a *Consumer Reports* study found that 7.5 million underage kids are on Facebook, and 5 million of these are ten years old or younger. While the sites can create rules, ultimately it is up to parents and guardians to monitor which sites their children use.

What about Facebook? Many parents don't realize that children aren't allowed to open Facebook accounts until the age of thirteen. Some parents allow kids to lie about their birth date to get a Facebook account. Facebook is difficult for many adults to navigate socially, let alone young kids, and allowing kids to fib about birth dates sets a bad example—two good reasons to just wait. When it is time to start a Facebook page, make a case that Mom and Dad must be Facebook "friends." It's one way to stay connected to what your child is doing online.

There are other social-networking sites that are designed specifically for children. Entering the words "children's social networking" into your search engine will yield information about sites that will allow you to determine if they meet the standards for your family. Spam filters, pop-up advertisement blocking, parental notification, and content filtering are important elements to look for when evaluating the appropriateness of a site for your child.

Here are a few to get you started: Poptropica.com, FunBrain.com, Funology .com, AmericanGirl.com, LearningPlanet.com, CBC.ca/Kids, PBSKids.org, TheIdeaBox.com, Lego.com, SIKids.com, ThomasAndFriends.com, Crayola .com, USMint.gov/education, Suessville.com, Kids.Discovery.com, and Kids .NationalGeographic.com.

Stimulating, Safe, and Fun

Many parents want the benefits of these amazing digital tools for their children. Modern technology offers an opportunity to have great family time together. Just as I advise families to watch television together, I would advise families to enjoy the Internet together. What hysterically funny YouTube video can you all enjoy? A blog about the weather in Siberia might stimulate a discussion about how kids who live there might deal with it. And, of course, postgame interviews with players from your favorite sports team offer a great opportunity for an enthusiastic conversation. Take the time to enjoy these things together.

AS KIDS GET OLDER

As children become young adults, you'll most likely loosen the restrictions surrounding online access, social networks, and smartphone use. Together, you will agree upon and set the limits. A little commitment from a teen can mean a lot when working on building trust and learning what will be expected of him as an adult. As your child becomes a teen or young adult, here are some issues you will want to discuss:

- **Costs:** Internet access, texts, downloads, minutes—none of these are free. Let your teen know what the fees are for the various services. After all, they'll be paying these once they're on their own. Some families ask teens to contribute to the monthly service cost; others expect reimbursement for overages.

- **Enforce limits:** Be ready to crack down if the limits you agreed to have been pushed or busted—and they will be! That's what teens do, so be prepared.

- **Illegal downloading:** This is a great time to discuss digital piracy, especially as it pertains to illegal downloads or file sharing. Sure, it's wrong because it's against the law, but you can also venture into discussions of ethics and the morality of taking another's work without paying for it.

- **Social networking:** Remind them that their social-network page can be viewed by anyone, including their teachers and potential future bosses. Anything online can end up recorded permanently and they need to be aware of this. Is that really the image they want to present forever?

- **NC-17:** Teens are naturally curious about sexuality, but as a parent you want that curiosity to stay healthy. While you might be able to control the sites your kids visit from your house, what about from their friends' houses? Talk to your kids about why you think certain sites are inappropriate and help them strategize how to "just say no" or even better, articulate their own reasons for having personal limits about watching explicit material.

- **Signs of trouble:** Keep an eye out for some of the hidden dangers of life online, such as cyber-bullying or online addiction. If you're suspicious, keep notes and watch for evidence to support your case. Meanwhile, make an extra effort to engage your teen in more face-to-face conversation and activities, and ask for help from a family health provider, treatment center, or law enforcement if you need it.

The Wireless Host

If you have a wireless network in your home, there are a few things consider when hosting others.

- If you maintain an open wireless network at your home or office, be sure that you have locked all files on your personal computer that you don't want to give anyone else access to.

- If you keep a closed or password-protected network, know your password or have it written down somewhere handy in case one of your guests requests it. It can be thoughtful to keep this information available on the desk of a guest room for overnight visitors.

- If you don't share your network information or keep a wireless network, know where the nearest wireless hotspot is in case your guests want to know where they can download e-mails, check stock reports, or update their Facebook page.

The Wireless Guest

Here are a few things to keep in mind when you find yourself wondering about how to join a wireless network in someone else's home.

- Check with your host before availing yourself of a home wireless network. Even if your phone connects automatically, it is polite to ask so that you do not exceed any limits or tax the data plan.

- If you see other local devices on an open network, don't snoop; stay out of other peoples files and programs.

- Similarly, when using an open network, check to be sure that you are not giving everyone else on the network access to files on your computer or mobile device if this matters to you.

- If a network is secured or password-protected, you may ask your host for a password to log on but be prepared to take no for an answer if your host doesn't want to give this information out.

- If someone has shared a network password with you, don't share it with anyone else.

Spouses and Significant Others

So many couples today feel like they never have time to talk about the little things, let alone spend quality time together. Jobs, kids, finances, social commitments, and a million other worthwhile obligations can all make it hard to find the time and energy for a meaningful conversation at the end of a long day. Mobile devices and texting are great for staying in touch with your spouse or significant other during the day and keeping that connection flourishing. But when you finally do sit down at night and your spouse spends two hours playing Angry Birds, devices can just add to the problem.

Set some guidelines together as a couple so that you, your spouse, and your mobile devices can live happily ever after.

- Try not to bookend your day with device check-ins.

- If you leave your device in the bedroom overnight, put it on silent mode or shut it off so that texts or e-mails received during the night don't wake your partner.

- Consider a "no-device-in-bed" rule—decide if this includes working in bed with a laptop, reading a bestseller on a tablet, and making to-do lists on your smartphone.

- Leave others out of it. Spending the evening texting or e-mailing brings another person into the room. Establish boundaries for uninterrupted couple or family time.

- Holidays and vacations. Holidays are a good time to keep your focus entirely on what's most important—the friends and family you are with. The same goes for vacations, though if one or both of you must be reachable for work, make a plan for when and how often you're available and share it with your office.

ELDERS ONLINE

Ten years ago it was considered pretty cool to have a grandparent who used e-mail. Today, almost every grandmother I know keeps in touch with her kids and grandkids through Facebook. Most seniors who are now retiring spent their work years using computers and the web. They are carrying those skills into retirement, keeping in touch with friends and family, studying new subjects, playing online games, and availing themselves of all the opportunities the online world brings to them. Some of these benefits include:

- E-mail, picture sharing, Skype or FaceTime, and social-network sites help seniors keep in touch with family and friends. This becomes even more meaningful when travel is no longer an option.

- If physical mobility is an issue, the Internet offers an array of entertainment choices, all from home.

- Electronic readers assist those with weakening eyesight—any book can become large-print by simply adjusting font size. Audiobooks and podcasts can be loaded onto a phone, tablet, or computer.

- Easy access to medical knowledge and assistance.

- Tablets are a good choice for some older folks, as they are less complicated to operate than a full desktop computer or laptop.

- Online dating is also popular with this demographic. (More on dating later in life in chapter 10, Dating.)

CARING FOR ELDERS

Today millions of Americans are not only raising children but are also caring
for aging parents. This double-whammy of family duty has led this group to be
dubbed the "sandwich generation." The good news is that it isn't just the children and parents benefitting from mobile devices and destinations, the elderly
are reaping the rewards as well.

If you're responsible for the care of an elderly person, whether it's a family
member or a good friend, getting them connected with a mobile phone, laptop,
tablet, or any other mobile device and teaching them how to use it can make
your life easier. Taking care of medical appointments, bills, banking, and other
day-to-day responsibilities can be easily accomplished via e-mail or online,
extending independence. Family and friends who can seem far removed from a
retirement community are now reachable at the push of a button.

Keep in mind, though, that if you provide your elders with a device and
online access, you are also responsible for teaching them (or at least finding
someone who will teach them) how to use it. This includes appropriate safety
precautions as well as mobile and social media manners. It's no good setting up

a Facebook account for Uncle John if he has no idea how to access it or if he gets online and starts messaging everyone in the family nonstop. Just as parents do this for children, so must adult children do this for parents and friends whom they help get online.

STAYING SAFE

The same safety advice we've been offering throughout this chapter applies for seniors as well:

- Avoid thinking that it would be rude not to respond to everyone who contacts you. If you don't know someone or their purpose for contacting you, you don't have to reply. In fact, you shouldn't.

- *Never* send your personal or financial data to someone you don't know. If you have initiated the contact (as when purchasing something online), you can give your credit card information, but be aware it still can be risky. (Of course, it can be risky when you use your credit card in person, too.)

- Be careful about where you store your passwords or any account numbers. Give a list of passwords and account numbers to a person you trust or the person to whom you have given durable power of attorney should they have to act on your behalf in case of emergency or death.

Seniors and Scams

Whether by envelope, landline, mobile phone, or computer, an entire industry has sprung up that targets seniors with scams designed to take their money. Many scams are run through e-mail or websites that are designed to look legitimate. They may appear official or personal or mimic something common like a sweepstakes or local service provider. Whatever the medium, the results can be disastrous. The advice is basic and the same from many sources: *never* give out personal or financial information in response to a request that you are unable to authenticate.

Banks, credit card companies, and legitimate businesses will work through websites that you can check out and call if necessary before giving out any information. A bank or credit card service will never call, e-mail, or text you to confirm your account number. If you are contacted by a legitimate organization in one of these ways, perhaps to alert you to fraud or problems with a card or account, you can always call the publicly listed number for that institution (or the number provided on the back of the card or statement) to confirm the veracity of a communication. And as always, take extra care with messages from strangers. Whether informing you of a "windfall" gift or begging you to wire money to someone stuck overseas (pick a reason—lost passport, credit cards, wallet), the aim is to part you from your money. And you'll never get it back.

10

DATING

Online dating statistics provide clear evidence that the digital dating trend has staying power. According to a 2012 study for MBAPrograms.org, the online dating industry has increased from a $900 million in 2007 to $1.9 billion in 2012. Since 2006, about 17 percent of married couples have met by using an online dating site. Couples who meet online and later get married date for an average of 18.5 months before getting married—married couples who met offline date for an average of 40 months before tying the knot.

Why is this medium so successful in helping people connect and fall in love? How does online dating work? Is its success limited to a demographic that is more comfortable online than with face-to-face encounters, or is the capability of dating-site matching algorithms truly the scientific achievement of the century?

If you believe the statistics above, then clearly a serious relationship can, and often does, begin online. Regardless, it's apparent that the rituals of meeting, socializing, and courting now take place in the digital space. Knowing how to behave while there is as essential now as knowing to bring along a chaperone on a first date was in 1922, when Emily Post's *Etiquette* was first published.

For some, the informality of communicating online provides a more relaxed getting-to-know-you phase. The perception of privacy and the comfort of online anonymity lead many to take chances and try things when dating online that they might normally be hesitant to try in person.

Many of the etiquette guidelines I'll share for dating online aren't that different from dating offline. From the time you set up your profile to the point when you are ready to arrange an in-person meeting, your conduct defines your image and can have a significant effect on your success. Your manners matter, and showcasing them online just requires some knowledge and self-confidence.

WHY TRY IT

What are the benefits to online dating? Some of the more popular answers include:

- You can get to know a potential date from the comfort of your own home.

- You can weed out the people who are obviously incompatible.

- It helps avoid first-date jitters, since you've already "met" online.

- You can take your search for a mate beyond the local pool.

- You can show your interest without the fear of face-to-face rejection.

WHERE IS EVERYONE HANGING OUT?

Here's a quick overview of some current industry-leading dating sites, how they describe themselves, and the number of registered users as of June 2012. You'll have to do some exploring and hang out at the sites where you feel the most comfortable.

- **Match.com.** Tagline: "Everyone knows someone who's found love on Match.com." With 32 million monthly visitors, Match.com is available in fifteen different languages and serves twenty-four countries.

- **eHarmony.com.** Tagline: "Most-trusted online dating site." Claims to be responsible for 5 percent of all US marriages. Has 20 million monthly visitors. For those looking for long-term relationships.

- **JDate.com.** Calls itself "the leading Jewish singles dating network and online community." Has 330,000 monthly visitors. Around for more than a decade, JDate provides other services to the Jewish online community, including a Jewish holiday calendar, synagogue directory, and Jewish magazine.

- **Zoosk.com.** Calls itself "the romantic social network." Claims to have more than 50 million monthly visitors. Younger, flirty. You can browse profiles without membership.

- **PlentyOfFish.com.** Tagline: "Responsible for more dates and more relationships than any other dating site." Has 32 million monthly visitors. A free site, this one has no bells and whistles.

- **Chemistry.com.** Tagline: "Get to know the person behind the profile." Has 1.5 million visitors per month. Extensive questionnaire should improve your odds of finding a good match.

- **OKcupid.com.** Tagline: "Join the best dating site on Earth." This quirky, fun, and, according to them, fastest-growing free dating site is currently very popular with the twentysomething set.

- **Craigslist.org.** While dating profiles appear on sites such as Craigslist, this is no different than responding to personals ads in the newspaper. Traditional dating sites may be a better bet.

GETTING STARTED

Use a reputable online dating site. Ask friends for recommendations. Protect your privacy by using the e-mail provided by the online service. Think about the interests that you'd like to build a relationship around. Dating sites have different ways to find people who share your interests, so it's OK to set up a profile on more than one site.

There are dating sites that segregate people by religion, age, income, brand affiliation, and many more attributes than you could imagine would matter. Some sites have in-depth personality diagnostic tools, designed to reveal information that could be helpful in determining good partners. Users don't evaluate one another so much as respond to suggestions identified by the service, which uses its own pairing criteria. Some people prefer the advantages of this model, as it allows information to be screened for veracity by the service. This simplifies the selection process that many find a burdensome and awkward first step.

FREE VERSUS FEE

Another thing for new users to consider is how a dating site makes money. There are two major models. One is a "pay for service" model, where users pay a subscription fee for full site access and services. The other model is paid for by advertisements, and members get to use the site for free. Because the cost of building feature-rich websites has fallen dramatically in recent years, the difference in quality and services offered by the two models has decreased.

There is value to a paid site that goes beyond the lack of pop-up ads and enhanced site features. An admission fee guarantees a certain degree of "buy-in" by all site participants that many find desirable. The temptation to troll a site, or play tricks with someone's emotions, is lessened when there is an upfront cost. Also, some "pay" sites verify certain information contained in profiles. For example, verification of income is just one attribute that might make the cost of admission to a "pay" service worth considering.

MOBILE DATING

Another type of relatively new dating service is one that helps connect two people who regularly frequent the same restaurants, museums, or coffee shops. These sites don't just use profile information to find matches, but can be enabled to use real-time and location information from GPS-equipped mobile devices as well. This can help two likely singles from the same dating network who happen to be in the same club or neighborhood on a given night find each other. Cruise ships and singles vacation resorts are starting to offer custom mobile apps to facilitate mix-and-mingle events as well as to establish private social networks for smaller retreat communities.

While the possibilities this opens up are exciting, the safety concerns involved in using services and devices that link personal information to real-time locations are potentially complex and very real. Think carefully before you employ one of these services, and be prepared to invest time in learning how to best use these powerful new tools safely.

The degree to which these services directly open one up to risky situations are debatable, and the risk versus reward for using them is really up to each person to determine for themselves. As always, a little common sense can go a long way when it comes to using these tools in the safest possible manner. (See also chapter 14, Digital Safety.)

PROTECTING YOUR PRIVACY, PROTECTING YOURSELF

There are several ways to protect yourself when you think about entering the world of online dating. One of the first is to set up an e-mail account exclusively to handle your dating e-mails. You might want to sequester your new dating e-mail account from your more established and preferred e-mail for family, friends, and colleagues.

By definition, when you start dating online, you are looking to meet new people and you will be communicating with people you don't know already. Consider a few privacy precautions as you begin, such as keeping this new stream of e-mails out of your work inbox.

CREATING YOUR PERSONAL PROFILE

Building an effective profile is the first step toward online dating success. Most users include elements such as pictures, videos, and other information about themselves, including age, gender, occupation, interests, and hobbies, as well as a brief description of their personality and what they are looking for in a partner or date.

Honesty remains one of the pillars of etiquette. It is essential that you are honest when you meet people online, too. This is the only way to foster a relationship over time. Remember that MBAPrograms.org survey? Other key findings showed that both women and men tend to lie about their physical appearance on online dating sites. Women claim to be 8.5 pounds thinner, and men claim to be two inches taller. Both men and women use profile pictures that are old so they appear younger. If only we all had a little more confidence in our appearance!

Leave any past indiscretions aside and adopt an policy of being honest with yourself. Don't present yourself in a way that is impossible to live up to.

ELEMENTS OF AN EFFECTIVE PROFILE

- The picture or video introduction is the most important element, so don't opt out. Text-heavy profiles tend to get ignored. Use a flattering picture that is not more than six months old.

- Your face should be clearly visible, and in the foreground. No landscapes, please, or group shots to keep them guessing. Take off the sunglasses and put down the pets. This is about you.

- If your profile lets you pick a username, choose something that fits your dating goals. Casual daters should not imply a search for life partners and those looking for marriage should avoid frivolities like "HotToTrot" or "SmokingGoodTime."

- Share interests: what books you are reading, movies you have seen recently, music you have in your player. Are you looking for a job, planning an adventure, or developing an art project?

- Depending on the service you select, you will be asked to provide information about what you are looking for in a partner: age, interests, education. Indicate if you are looking for "someone like me," "someone to challenge me," "someone to support me," "someone to date casually." Whatever it is, let people know what you are looking for.

- And finally . . . provide suggestions for the best way to get in touch with you. Ask a question to answer in a first reply, or request a mention of something specific from the profile to help get a conversation started.

Boomer Dating

A large and growing portion of the singles dating pool in America is between the ages of forty-eight and sixty-six. Just as they invest, watch TV, and talk to their kids online, boomers date online as well. Whether divorced, widowed, or simply still single, dating online is both popular and successful for boomers.

While many boomers need no help in the area of technology, any who do should approach online dating with a spirit of fun and curiosity. While all of the advice in this chapter applies to boomers, here are a few additional tips to get started:

- If you're feeling technologically challenged, ask for the help of more knowledgeable friends or family members and have them guide you through the basics of finding websites and setting up an account.
- Bounce ideas off of other friends who are dating and share stories as you go through the process of requesting and screening dates. A dating friend or buddy will make the successes more fun and the failures easier to take.
- Take heart from the fact that you are not alone. There are many other people going through the same process.

MAKING CONTACT

Either party may initiate contact with someone who seems interesting or whose profile is attractive. Once a contact has been made, it is up to the users to engage each other and find out if there is enough there to warrant a continuing online exchange or an in-person meeting.

HOW TO SAY "THANKS, BUT NO THANKS"

If you were approached in a bar by someone you weren't that interested in, you wouldn't just ignore them, would you? Most likely you would think of a polite way to let them down, for example, "Sorry, I'm not looking for a relationship" or "I've already got a boyfriend/girlfriend." That sort of thing. Unfortunately, you can't get away with these excuses online because, well, let's face it, you *are* looking for a relationship and that's why you're there.

So if someone contacts you and they aren't your type or don't tick your boxes, don't just ignore them. Respond to them in a way you would like to be responded to. Simply be polite and let them down gently by saying "Sorry, you're out of my age range" or "I'm looking for someone who lives a little closer" and then wish them well in their continued search.

Tips for Connecting

Whether it's in your profile or when you are communicating with potential dates, keep it positive.

	DO THIS!	NOT THAT!
Post a Picture	A current headshot that represents your true and best self	A pic that is "−10X": you ten years ago and ten pounds lighter
State Your Goals	I am looking for someone who knows how to have fun.	I need someone who isn't a drag
Talk About Your Interests	I am someone who likes to be active outdoors; hiking, camping, gardening	People who watch TV annoy me
Interest People, Don't Scare Them	I am passionate about health and nutrition	I only eat fresh-picked greens and locally harvested roots
Be Open, but Don't Be Desperate	I am looking for a seriously wonderful relationship	I was supposed to get married three years ago and am three years behind on my life plan
Be Quirky, but Don't Be a Fool	For fun I like to watch Saturday-morning cartoons and eat sugared cereal	I live with my parents and collect action figures and try to date online because I can't leave the house without my Superman costume
Be Honest	I have two great kids and live in the Cincinnati metro area	I am the twenty-seven-year-old vision you are dreaming of, currently a dancer in NYC

FIRST CONTACT

Most first contacts are made through in-site messaging or e-mail, followed by a series of exchanges—or not, as the case may be. Here are some tips for successful beginnings:

- Use salutations and closings when you are initiating contact: Dear, Hello, Greetings; Sincerely, Best, and Warmly.

- Mention something specific from the profile: "I see that you live with twenty-four cats."

- Introduce yourself and mention a common interest: "I am a big pet fan myself."

- Avoid clichés: "This is my first time trying online dating."

- Expand your pool: Try reaching out to someone who might not be exactly what you think you are looking for but who seems interesting.

INTERMEDIATE STEPS: TALKING ON THE PHONE

After some initial e-mails back and forth, you may be ready for the next step, usually a phone call. This is a more personal step in the getting-to-know-you process than e-mails. Here are some tips for starting out on the right foot.

- Suggest a call, don't just send your number. Ask, "Would it be all right if I sent you my phone number?"

- Be prepared with a few questions.

- Don't overdo it; a few questions, then ask to call again.

- Be positive and polite.

- Take it slowly. You don't need to ask for a date on the first call.

FIRST MEETINGS

It is normal for a first date to follow a series of e-mail exchanges or phone calls. It is not uncommon to plan to meet at a social gathering that includes others or to bring along a friend, so don't be surprised or offended if someone suggests this for a first date. There are a few general dating safety tips for first dates that are important to review for dating online as well as off. (See also "Meeting Offline" in chapter 14, Digital Safety, pages 214–218.) Let's start with the big three.

ONLINE DATING SAFETY—THE BIG THREE

While these tips may apply especially to women, men and women of all orientations should be willing to accommodate any of these parameters if they are suggested.

1. Make it public. Be sure to schedule a first meeting where you are comfortable and could get help with a bad situation should it develop.

2. Tell a friend. Be sure someone knows where you are going and who you are meeting, including their dating profile name: for example, "SurfDog" from OKCupid.com. Let your friend know when you will check in and what to do if you don't call.

3. Use extreme caution when drinking alcohol if you plan to drink at all. While having a drink is a common dating activity, it affects judgment at a time when good judgment is critical. It is not necessary to drink on a first date and in many instances is inadvisable. If you do choose to drink, keep your drink in sight at all times and watch your personal limit.

MORE TIPS FOR SAFE AND FUN FIRST DATES

- Go ahead. You know you want to. Google them first. Welcome to the information age, where it is not snooping to see what comes up when you Google the name of a potential date. In fact, it is a reasonable part of due diligence. If what you learn is off-putting, you can end it, or at least be forewarned. You may find something cool and intriguing that can advance your conversation. For example, "So, I have a confession to make. I looked you up online and saw that you were a three-time gold medalist in boxing. Are you still in training?"

- Stay in control of your own transportation. This may mean driving yourself or keeping cab fare and a taxi number handy. Don't get into a car with someone you don't already know and trust. Don't accept a ride home if you do not intend to reveal your home address.

- Be sure that you have a phone handy.

- Consider going Dutch to keep everyone on an equal footing.

- Trust your instincts. Listen to the little voices that tell you something is "too good to be true" or "isn't quite right here."

WHO PAYS?

Early in a relationship, many people prefer to pay their own way to avoid putting themselv   t. It is perfectly reasonable to suggest that each person   ring the get-to-know-you phase of a relationship. Disc   hould be open, candid, and honest. If you have any ques   who is paying, the sooner you ask or bring them up, the   meal when the check arrives is not the time for negotiations. Unpleasant surprises at this moment are best avoided by knowing who is paying before you go.

Traditionally, host and guest roles dictate that the person who does the inviting picks up the bill. When men always did the inviting, it became the norm for the man to pay for the date. Today, women are just as likely to be the ones doing the asking. Gentlemen, if you prefer to play the traditional role on a first date, that is OK. However, if your date wants to split the bill, you should honor her wish.

Helpful First Date Dos and Don'ts

- Do be on time. Don't keep your date waiting.
- Do dress for the occasion. This isn't the time to flaunt your Saturday hanging-out-at-home wardrobe.
- Do turn off your phone for a few hours. Taking a call isn't going to make you seem more successful or important.
- Do remember your table manners. Chew with your mouth closed, don't talk with food in your mouth, and don't wolf down your food.
- Do be thoughtful and considerate. Men, remember "ladies first," but don't overdo the chivalry: a dozen roses is too much for the first date.
- Do be yourself and look for people who will make *you* happy. Don't try to change yourself completely to make someone else interested.
- Do have fun. Don't complain.

BREAKING IT OFF

Ending a relationship is difficult and should be handled with care. This is true whether you are the dumpee, the dumper, or the relationship is ending because of mutually agreed upon and understood reasons. Whatever role you are playing, the end of a relationship can feel awkward and confusing. The best test of manners and grace comes when the pressure is on and the situation is difficult. This is one of the most important times to behave well and maintain your personal integrity.

ENDING IT WELL

Because it can be painful, there is a tendency to want to avoid the end of a relationship. Here are some general guidelines to ensure that you take as much care with ending a relationship as you have put into building it.

- If someone you have never reached out to or made any acknowledgment of is repeatedly trying to contact you, it is not necessary to explain why you are not responding.

- If you have initiated or replied to a contact, it is important to acknowledge if you are ending that connection, however brief.

- If you have gone so far as to meet someone but are not planning on doing so again, you should acknowledge the choice you have made when you next make contact. "I enjoyed meeting you, but I didn't feel we had that much in common. I wish you the best."

- A true breakup of a relationship that has lasted more than a few dates should be done in person, or at least on the phone.

- Don't hide behind an electronic device or a change in Facebook status. People's feelings are involved; showing due consideration and care for the feelings of others is a critical component of good manners.

WHEN IT ENDS BEFORE YOU ARE READY

If you are the one being rejected, strive for grace and poise as you hear the news. Accepting that someone is no longer interested can be difficult, but it is something that everyone goes through. I have a good friend who likes to say "Never trust someone in a relationship who has never had his or her heart broken." What he means is that going through heartbreak teaches us about both the fragility and the resiliency of the human heart. He thinks this type of lesson leads to a deeper understanding of what is at stake in an intimate relationship, and I think there is some value to this insight. Nobody wants to be with someone who is not interested in them, so be grateful that the other person is letting you know that this match is not going to work for them or you.

Who Gets the Friends?

Friendship does not have to be a zero-sum game. Just like a divorce in real life, a breakup or divorce in a social-media environment affects the friends and contacts of both parties. There is no set rule saying who gets which friends. In the best of cases, everyone can still be friends. However, when things go badly and battle lines are drawn, let your friends self-select which person they will stay in touch with.

ONLINE RELATIONSHIPS

Affairs of the heart are hard to define. The very language we use to describe emotion distinguishes it from the logical and reasoning faculties of the mind. Asking to generate a definition of a romantic relationship is asking for trouble. Romance is romance wherever one finds it—even online. We have talked about how an online friendship can be just as valid, deep, and personal as one conducted in "real life." The same can be true of an online romance. It might never need to move offline to be true and totally fulfilling. Establishing an online romance might be the final goal for many who date online. If this is what you are looking for, it is good to be clear about your intention early on, as this is not the norm for most dating communities.

SUCCESS

So, when your online meeting turns into a truly committed relationship, it's time to take down your profile and close your account.

Getting Past the Awkward Factor

One of the classic questions about online dating is how to deal with the profile that helped you meet someone you are now dating. Taking it down sends a clear message that you think you may no longer be available or at least are no longer actively looking to meet someone new. Doing this too soon could be seen as moving too fast. Leaving it up for too long risks appearing like you can't move a relationship forward. It is a pivotal moment in the online dating experience that nearly everyone wrestles with.

The right moment to take down a dating site profile will be different for each person and for each couple. One adviser I consulted suggested it can fun for a new couple to take down their profiles together when they hit the stage in the relationship when they are ready to do this. It may not work for everyone, but I like the idea.

Precisely because questions about the status of a romantic relationship are so fraught, many people avoid posting their relationship status on social networks like Facebook until they know they are in an established and committed relationship. The question of when you change your relationship status can be just as touchy at the end of a relationship as at the beginning. Rather than deal with this every time a relationship begins and ends, many people wisely avoid relationship-status posting altogether.

WEDDINGS

If your relationship that began online has led to wedding bells, and we know that many do, you will find that technology can be invaluable as you plan your big day: creating a pinboard for wedding dresses or floral inspiration; viewing venues and menus online; using e-mail to keep parents, attendants, and vendors up to speed; building a wedding website to post directions, ceremony information, and links to your registry; organizing guest lists and making seating charts. Your entire wedding can be planned online. One particularly tempting area of the online wedding world is the e-invitation.

WEDDING EVITES: YES OR NO?

Q. "Is it OK to send wedding invitations by e-mail or post them on my wedding website?"

A. This is one place where I advise a more traditional approach. It is true that weddings today are all about personalization and a customized experience, but before making your decision, consider these questions: Does your mom's cousin Alma use or check her e-mail regularly? Do you have everyone's up-to-date e-mail address? And most important: Does an evite really reflect the very special nature of a wedding? To my mind, the answer to this last question is a very strong no.

Be particularly careful about using your digital social network to announce your upcoming wedding. Don't let an announcement on Facebook be misconstrued as an invitation. Worse yet, don't use your personal page to do your actual inviting. Once people have been invited, a wedding website can be a great option for coordinating events and schedules, planning bride and groom parties, listing registries, posting travel and hotel recommendations, and a thousand other things I am not creative enough to anticipate. From guest-created set lists replacing hackneyed DJ fare to setting up places for guests to send and share their best pictures, I keep hearing about all of the ways that new technology is making weddings more fun for everyone. Just be sure that at this important seminal event you don't leave anyone behind as you cruise down the high-tech superhighway to your new life.

11

THE WORK WORLD

For almost everyone, work today involves technology. Whether you're a PR executive using social media to maintain global brands or a building contractor staying on top of supply orders from a job site with a smartphone, technology helps you get the job done. Even professionals who might not traditionally have been considered tech-oriented, such as farmers, artists, or athletes, use mobile devices and interact online on a daily basis as part of their professional lives.

In your career, the stakes are high when it comes to using these tools well. A friend will forgive you for the occasional mobile manners lapse, and a spouse will talk to you (hopefully!) about any faux pas that you make on Facebook. But a colleague, boss, client, prospect, customer, vendor, or supplier might not give you the benefit of the doubt or talk to you about a problem they have with your behavior. That doesn't mean they didn't notice and draw conclusions, however.

More than ever, it's important to think about how others in business will perceive your actions, be it in person, with how you use your mobile devices, or in how you present yourself online.

Your Professional Image Online

A big part of stepping into social media for work is minding your image, both for your own sake and for your employer's. Like it or not, people will judge you on your online image. So whether it's Google searches, LinkedIn profiles, Facebook pages, or tweets, be sure you're sending the right message about your professionalism and personal judgment.

Google Yourself

Thanks to the Internet, information is the standard currency of the twenty-first century, and it's a safe bet you can be found with a simple Google search of your name. For many, an image search will produce photos, too. Some of this information you won't be surprised to find; other references might be unexpected— a photo posted by a friend, a blog comment from years ago that still gets top search billing thanks to the search-engine optimization by the hosting site. People can find out all kinds of information about you, and it's likely that at some point interviewers, prospects, clients, and bosses will Google you.

Given that, be proactive and Google yourself on a regular basis. And while you're at it, try several other search engines such as Bing and Yahoo!. Then you'll know exactly what people can learn about you or your organization when they do a search for your name. Be sure you're comfortable with what you find, because if you found it, others might stumble across it too. Online reputation cleanup services like Reputation.com can manipulate search results so that positive elements score higher on searches, and negative results are pushed down the list, but they can do little to actually make them go away and often cost a pretty penny. But you can at least be prepared by knowing what is out there, and then plan to keep a sharper eye on what you allow to become publicly available in the future.

LinkedIn

LinkedIn is the first and largest social network designed for professional and business online networking. Founded in 2003, it currently has more than 100 million users. LinkedIn offers a suite of features designed to connect business colleagues new and old, enable job postings and searches, and host conversations about business-related questions. The user's profile picture is the primary visual in this text-heavy medium. However, when users post links/URLs, the related image will appear on the dashboard. Users ask to "Link In" or connect to other members. Think of LinkedIn as a communal contact management system combined with an online résumé.

WHO SHOULD YOU CONNECT TO?

Most users create a profile and then ask colleagues and coworkers to connect with them. Users can request to connect with clients, friends, former coworkers, and interesting acquaintances through a LinkedIn request. If the person you wish to connect with doesn't have a profile, you can invite them to join if you have their e-mail address.

LinkedIn Versus Facebook

LinkedIn is primarily a networking and shared contact-management tool designed for working professionals. Facebook is really more of an online location where people hang out and socialize, although it has become a major marketing tool. Both communities require membership, but LinkedIn is searchable by those who are not members of the community, while Facebook is not. Know that if you keep your contact information as part of your public LinkedIn profile, it is viewable by anyone who is searching the web.

Here are five tips for maintaining a positive LinkedIn profile:

1. Make sure your profile is an extension of your personal brand. Consider LinkedIn your online résumé that potential colleagues, clients, and employers can easily access.

2. The more information, the better. Don't be stingy with your résumé information—you want people to be able to see how amazing you are. Corporate recruiters and other HR-type professionals can search LinkedIn to find the "right" people. Make sure your attributes, skills, and experience are fleshed out in your profile.

3. Don't stretch the truth and give yourself capabilities you don't have or take credit for work you didn't really do.

4. Use a professional—or at least good-looking—head shot. Avatars, cartoon characters, tropical vacation shots, and pictures of your dog are for Facebook. If you want to be seen as an expert in your field, you have to look like an expert on your profile page.

5. Join or create "Groups." Relationships don't just happen—they take effort and nurturing, and groups are a way to interact with other LinkedIn users with similar interests.

MONITORING YOUR ONLINE PROFILES

Regardless of whether you're a member of LinkedIn, Facebook, or other social networking sites such as Google+, Tumblr, or Pinterest, be sure to protect your professional image by using the right networks for the right purposes. Also be sure to:

- Visit each site you use regularly and look at what is on your page and what others are saying about you.

- Set preferences to notify you when you are tagged or mentioned in a post or tweet, receive a friend or connection request, or are sent a message. You can set up alerts to notify you about new content connected with your name served through Google searches, as well. Monitor these notifications carefully if, for some reason, you aren't visiting a site regularly to catch anything you need to address.

- Check to see which parts of your profile are viewable by strangers and adjust any settings as needed.

- Keep your profile information up-to-date, especially your employer, title, job description, and work experience.

- Ask a friend or a colleague at work to look at your pages with you and give you an outsider's impression of what works and what might not. Just as a friend can be a big help in choosing the right outfit, they can help you with your online presentation as well.

- If you don't use Facebook for business contacts, consider setting up a LinkedIn account so that you have somewhere to connect with colleagues and other professional contacts who are interested in net-working with you online for business purposes.

TROUBLESHOOTING FACEBOOK AND WORK

Here are some of the top questions that can crop up when the line between Facebook and your work life blur:

Q. My boss sent me a friend request, and I'm nervous about ignoring it. What should I do?

A. You could choose to ignore it and invite her to connect on LinkedIn instead. Or you could make sure your page is appropriate for her to see and accept the request. You can always adjust what she can see or write with your privacy settings. Which option you choose is up to you; the key is that you think about how she might react to your choice, and that you ultimately make a connection with her somewhere.

Q. A friend just posted a bunch of pictures from our college graduation weekend almost ten years ago and tagged me in them. Though they're hysterical, they're also embarrassing; what do I do?

A. It is OK and may even be advisable to untag yourself from these pictures. Next, contact your friend and ask him to remove any pictures that you are really uncomfortable with, since untagging them won't remove them from Facebook, just from being linked to your profile and labeled with your name.

Q. I'm friends with a coworker on Facebook. I noticed a message someone posted on his wall about how sorry they are to hear about his mother passing away. He hasn't mentioned this to me; what should I do?

A. If he doesn't take the message mentioning her death down right away, then it's probably OK to act on this news. Pick a quiet moment to mention that you happened to read about it on Facebook, and are so sorry to hear about his loss. Offer condolences and a card as you normally would. (For more on condolences, see chapter 13, Tough Times.)

Q. I noticed a coworker on Facebook posted something rude about our supervisor. I know she is not a Facebook friend of his, but everyone else in the office is. What do I do?

A. You could choose a private moment to lightly mention to your coworker that she might want to be careful about posting anything negative about work, as it's sure to get around with so many colleagues being connected. You could also just let it go and file it under "good to know" if you don't know her very well. Either way, don't gossip about it or bring it to your supervisor's attention—that would be tattling.

TWITTER

It is amazing how normally rational, thinking people fail to heed advice they would routinely give to others. One place they do this with alarming frequency is Twitter posts. From former congressman Anthony Weiner to Gilbert Gottfried (the former Aflac duck voice) to Miami Heat owner Micky Arison, the jaw-dropping examples of stupid mistakes keep rolling in. Whether they think a Twitter post will only be noticed by close followers or they succumb to the immediacy of winging off a few short words without thinking first, the ramifications of a mistake can travel far and have serious consequences.

Consider the case of James Andrews, a Ketchum PR account executive and vice president, who tweeted this about Memphis, Tennessee, while he was there to visit a major client—as in FedEx major:

"True confession but I'm in one of those towns where I'd scratch my head and say 'I'd rather die than live here.'"

Big mistake. Before he arrived at his client's headquarters, the client had already seen the tweet. Needless to say, the client wanted an explanation. While the issue was eventually settled, his tweet not only hurt the client relationship but could have caused damage to his position within Ketchum as well.

Once you put a comment out there, be it a tweet, status update, or blog comment, it's fair game for anyone to see. Unfortunately, the ease with which tweets can be written and posted makes them prone to rash, quick comments—comments you may wish you hadn't made. Think before you post a tweet. Let it sit for a few minutes, and then go back and read it. If you have any doubt at all, ask a colleague you trust for his opinion. That moment's hesitation could save you a lot of grief.

And it goes without saying that you need to know how to use a new medium before you dive in. The reach of Twitter in particular is enormous, so be careful. Ignorance can mean the difference between sending a DM (direct message) correctly or having it go out as a tweet to your whole network. Apps and programs may be billed as intuitive, but save yourself some embarrassment (and maybe your job) and read the "How To" guide first.

YOUR COMPANY'S ONLINE IMAGE

Just like people, companies have Facebook, LinkedIn and Twitter profiles, websites, and blogs. Marketing departments are discovering all of the ways they can utilize social media, as are public relations professionals. If your company has a social media presence, ask about company policies for using and participating in it.

Slander and libel rules still apply online, as do privacy agreements and copyrights, but in the age of WikiLeaks and international digital piracy, it can be a good idea to have an ironclad set of in-house policies that spell out what constitutes proper use of the company's social media presence and consequences for inappropriate use. The guidelines also should include the following three directions:

1. Be transparent. An employee responding to comments on a company blog or social media page should declare their official capacity in a forthright and public manner. Whenever operating in an official capacity on behalf of a company, it is important to identify yourself and your purpose.

2. Anyone being *paid,* and this includes receiving free products, to promote a product or brand online should be upfront about this.

3. When offering reviews on an independent rating service like Yelp or using a platform like Tumblr or even Wikipedia to promote a brand, be sure to follow all of the rules for posting to that site.

TEN TIPS FOR PROFESSIONAL SOCIAL MEDIA POSTS

1. Truncated sentences or text abbreviations such as OMG, LMAO, LMK are one thing on Twitter, but when you have the space, write in complete sentences and avoid text abbreviations.

2. Proofread for spelling, grammar, and word choice. When you misspell a word, use poor grammar, or misuse a word, readers notice and it suggests that you are careless.

3. Emoticons—☺ ☹ ☺—are fun in personal communications but need to be industry- and situation-appropriate when posting to your company's social media page, and even then should be used sparingly if it all.

4. Know how to use @, RT, MT, via, and so on. (See also "Know the Code," in chapter 5, Twitter, pages 68–70.)

5. Emotional content can be difficult, so stick to the facts.

6. Always review before you post. Don't post when you are angry or overly emotional. Let it simmer for a few minutes and then read it

one more time before you do something that can't be undone. If you need to take more than a few minutes to regain your composure, do so rather than make a mistake you might regret later.

7. Be conscious of your tone. We can hear tone of voice when someone is speaking to us, but we also can hear the tone in someone's writing. If you want to hear your tone of voice in your writing, read your post out loud.

8. Don't overpost; it becomes like spam to those who follow your company, and you run the risk of annoying, and thus losing, followers.

9. Engage with any criticism or feedback. While it's fine to give your company's point of view on the matter, acknowledge concerns and avoid defensiveness or anger in your response.

10. Credit or attribute all content that you don't produce yourself.

If you have any questions about a post or a tweet, be sure to check the social-media policies at your place of employment.

MANAGING YOUR COMPANY'S TWITTER ACCOUNT

Software is available that can help you get the most out of Twitter. Both HootSuite and TweetDeck are popular free platforms for managing Twitter from a laptop or desktop computer. They can be a big help when tracking a couple of different topics, and can assist in managing relationships with a growing list of followers. They also allow you to schedule tweets ahead of time (very convenient!). If you preload your Twitter feed, don't forget to check in to respond to new comments.

Ethical Considerations in Marketing and Promotions

As I said before, if you work for a company and are commenting on your company blog or website, you should identify yourself as being employed by that company. It is so important to maintaining a good reputation, if you are being paid to market or promote a product and are discussing it online, you should acknowledge this. Posting online using a pseudonym is one thing to be very careful of in a professional capacity. It's fine if you are simply looking to add your opinion to the debate. It is not fine if you have an agenda and try to hide it. It is hard to build business relationships on deception. Simply identify yourself and your official capacity, and then it's perfectly OK to add your two cents. (See also "Disclosure" in chapter 6, Online Communities, page 91.)

MOBILE DEVICES IN THE WORKPLACE

As I mentioned in chapter 2, Mobile Devices, smartphones, tablets, laptops—they're all just tools, and tools can be used appropriately or inappropriately. Technology isn't the problem; people are. At work, how you use and manage your mobile devices will affect your success.

In our jobs we often work within two competing expectations: to be constantly available to anyone who tries to reach us, and to focus only on the task at hand or the person we are with. Walking this tricky line isn't about only one of those expectations; it's about responding in a way that's appropriate to each situation, each time. The key is to control your mobile device, rather than be controlled by it.

SMARTPHONES

Smartphones are great tools and actually can enhance productivity. You are more reachable, which, while it can be a problem if it leads to work creep, can help keep the wheels of business moving.

- You can respond quickly to a request from a client or prospect.

- You can call while on the way to a meeting to inform them you are delayed and will be a few minutes late. Much better than letting them cool their heels wondering where you are and when you'll show up.

- You can check e-mails and respond quickly when necessary.

- You have relatively instant access to your office and colleagues when you need it.

The key to using the smartphone successfully is to be in control of it. Far too often people get a mobile phone and then feel compelled to always respond to it even if it means interrupting people they are with.

When I conduct a business-etiquette seminar for a company, inevitably the person hiring me has a particular issue the company wants addressed. Not surprisingly, one of the top issues I hear is: "Tell them not to use their smartphones during a meeting." One CEO at a consulting firm was adamant about solving this problem. His employees were so addicted to their smartphones that they were constantly checking them during meetings.

When I customized the seminar for this client, I built in five moments where the point about no cell phones in meetings could be made. Amazingly, just as I reached the point when I brought the issue up for the third time, lo and behold, a phone began ringing. People started looking around; no one was taking responsibility. Finally, one consultant sheepishly reached into her handbag and turned off the phone. Of course, by the time she reached into the bag, the ribbing she got from the other participants was far more effective than anything I could have said.

Later, after the fifth time that I raised the phone issue during the seminar, I looked over at the CEO and asked, "Have I made it clear enough for you?" He smiled and replied, "I think you have." I asked him that question not as a joke but as a final emphasis of the point. The company was serious, and the CEO was serious. The culture at this company had to change. No more smartphone use during meetings.

(For general tips on mobile-device use, see chapter 2, Mobile Devices. For mobile-device boundaries between work and personal life, see chapter 12, When Worlds Collide.)

TURN IT OFF OR USE A SILENT OR VIBRATE MODE.

The tried-and-true normal ringtone of a smartphone is disruptive enough. But when the Lone Ranger charges through an office or Beethoven's fifth symphony *dah-dah-dah daaaaah*s for the fifth time, your colleagues are not going to be able to stay focused on their work. Give your workmates a break and use the silent or vibrate mode at work.

BEWARE OF "PHONE VOICE"

What is one of the top complaints workers have about colleagues in the work-place? It's "phone voice." For some reason we think we have to talk louder when we're on a phone. Well, you don't.

On a regular office phone, you can hear your own voice through the earpiece, but people still talk too loudly. A smartphone doesn't have a feed-back loop from the mouthpiece to the earpiece, so you don't hear your own voice through the earpiece. Result: you talk louder; those around you are annoyed.

WHEN YOUR PHONE RINGS IN A MEETING

The absolute worst thing you can do if your phone starts ringing in a meeting is to look around and pretend it's not your phone. You're hoping the ringing will stop before the rest of the attendees zero in on you as the culprit.

Not going to happen.

Your best bet is to grab your phone as quickly as possible and do whatever your phone requires to stop the ringing. Then turn it off completely. Don't look to see who is calling before deciding to switch it off. If it wasn't supposed to have been on, you don't need to know who was calling. Plus, checking it sends the message "Is this caller more important than all of you?" to others in the room. If the presenter is looking at you, offer a quick apology.

INTRODUCE NEW TECHNOLOGY

Psyched to use that new iPad to take notes in a meeting? It's not a bad idea to let people know what you're doing when you introduce a new mobile device to a meeting. "I'm going to take some notes on my iPad today," or "I'll have my laptop out to monitor breaking news on this issue during the meeting." When you bring a new device into the equation and people don't know what you're doing, they may make negative assumptions—as in, maybe you're goofing off. Let them know upfront how you plan to use the technology, and then keep your usage to the purpose you stated.

SET CLEAR MEETING EXPECTATIONS

If mobile-device distraction is a problem in your office, when you're the meeting organizer it's important to set expectations for mobile-device use verbally. In fact, it's good regardless. Better to say "If everyone could please put their BlackBerrys away" upfront than to have to single out someone who's checking e-mail later—it makes it much easier to raise an eyebrow at a culprit if they've been given fair warning. This also works well for focusing device usage when one is needed for the task at hand. For example, "Please minimize all screens on your laptops that don't pertain to the meeting. Thanks."

MANAGING UP

What about when the problem isn't you, but your boss? Good mobile manners should go both ways, and employees often feel frustrated by higher-ups who aren't paying attention in meetings because they are checking e-mails on a smartphone. They feel their hands are tied, and sometimes, especially if they aren't the meeting leader, they are. But in some cases, there might be a way to say something. There are two ways to go: when you're the meeting leader, start by following the policy in the paragraph above and ask that everyone put away their mobile devices when the meeting opens. If you have a good relationship with your boss, you might rib him a little and say jokingly, "That means you, Bob!" Or if you feel certain the relationship could handle a more frank conversation, say privately, "Bob, your input is really valuable and I'd like to get the most out of your time during meetings. Would you mind putting the BlackBerry away?"

Another approach would be to acknowledge the role a boss or supervisor plays in establishing workplace culture. Ask them to help you set the standards that make for the best meetings by refraining from using mobile devices themselves.

THE 50/10 RULE

Employees need to be available, but you want their undivided attention. Help them help you by giving them a break. For every 50 minutes of meeting time, give a 10-minute e-mail and call break. The numbers are just a suggestion; what matters is that attendees can focus on the meeting knowing they'll have regular opportunities to check in on other priorities.

MULTITASKING

The jury is still out on whether we can multitask well or not, and with the rise of a new generation raised on multitasking, this question won't go away anytime soon. When it comes to multitasking on a mobile device while in the presence of others, my take is simple: even if you really could multitask brilliantly, the impression you give to the people you're with is that you aren't paying attention to them. And that perception can cost you far more than getting ahead on a few e-mails ever would have gained you.

SMARTPHONES AREN'T A FOURTH EATING UTENSIL

It's a familiar sight: businesspeople walk up to their table in a restaurant and immediately take their smartphones out and set them on the table. As my cousin Anna likes to say, phones are not a fourth eating utensil! It's bad enough to check a smartphone during a regular meeting; using a smartphone at a business lunch or dinner can be a deal-breaker. Business meals are about building and furthering business relationships, and people don't like to be ignored. When you answer your phone or read and possibly even respond to a text message or e-mail, you are telling the person you are with that your phone and the person on the other end of it are more important than he is. That is a message that is remembered long after the call is completed.

The one exception is if you inform the person you are with that you are expecting an important call and will excuse yourself to take it in the lobby when the time comes. Place your phone on vibrate so you can quietly leave without disturbing the other diners when your phone rings.

IS IT **OK** TO MIX BUSINESS WITH BUSINESS?

At a cocktail mixer for work, is it OK to check your smartphone in between talking to other guests? Yes, but step into the lobby. Even though you aren't ignoring a conversation partner, you're not participating in the event like everyone else when you pull out your mobile device and start checking in with people who are not present.

SENDING THE RIGHT MESSAGE

The immediacy and convenience of texting, IMing, and e-mailing have obvious competitive advantages for fast-paced work environments. However, since it is not an established type of business communication, texting might be perceived by some coworkers and supervisors as not being work related or, even if it is work related, not as a professional way of representing yourself in business. This goes double whenever you're texting with or in the presence of clients, prospects, higher-ups, or anyone from outside your industry or generation.

BEWARE OF AUTOCORRECT!

When texting or e-mailing from a mobile device with autocorrect (it's like spell check, only it changes any word it thinks you've misspelled with the word it thinks you meant), always, always, *always* reread your message before you send it. Autocorrect can make bizarre or hilarious errors when it attempts to correct your typing—and sometimes it makes disastrously inappropriate errors. Please, reread!

> ### If You've Lost Your Phone
>
> If you lose your work phone, contact your IT department immediately. Often, they will have the ability to ping your phone and wipe it completely. Phones like the iPhone 4 series have a feature that lets you find the phone, have the phone emit a tone to help locate, it or send a signal to the phone to wipe it clean so you can protect any confidential information that might be on it.

WORK LAPTOPS AND COMPUTERS

Most of what needs to be said about using a laptop has been covered in chapter 2, Mobile Devices, but there are a few work-related topics that are worth covering.

PRIVACY

You may think of your work computer as your private computer, but it's not. It belongs to your company. All the information and content you keep on it is subject to your company's examination. Many businesses require that employees share all passwords and accounts that are run through company systems. Beyond official policy it is important to remember that there may be information technology professionals who have access to the content in personal e-mails sent on company accounts.

VIDEO CONFERENCES AND WEBINARS

From Skype to iChat to FaceTime to GoToMeeting, to name just a few, video conferencing is on the rise. Consider the following when organizing or participating in a video conference or webinar:

- Check connection speed and site performance before an important meeting or call. Dropped connections break the meeting flow and waste time.

- You may need to do a trial run if you have never used a certain system before. In fact, be sure to plan for time to test the exact system that you will be using before you need to rely on it.

- Find a private space to conduct the meeting or call.

- Think about the visual background your audience might see and minimize any background sounds they might hear. Keep your backgrounds quiet, clean, and neat to avoid distraction.

- Be on time. If you're the organizer, that means opening the connection before the start time so everyone can log in or on and be ready to go by the start time.

- Identify everyone who is involved and participating, as well as anyone sitting or listening in.

- Take care with your appearance. Be dressed and groomed as you would for any face-to-face meeting.

- Refrain from fidgeting, doodling, or other behaviors that indicate boredom or distraction. People can hear you tapping your pencil; they can see you texting on your smartphone.

12

WHEN WORLDS COLLIDE

No matter what your profession or job, you probably use a mobile device or personal computer as part of your daily work routine. The average corporate employee sends and receives more than one hundred e-mails in a day according to John Freeman, author of *The Tyranny of E-mail*. One of the most sought-after job skills right now in today's information economy is the ability to learn and master new software and devices. Success in landing a job in a very competitive market depends in part on job candidates knowing how to use technology appropriately—it can make all the difference in both getting and keeping a job.

Yet it's just as important to create personal boundaries for the use of these devices. Today's professional is expected to manage two kinds of "creeping" behaviors: one is the tendency for personal activities and communications to creep into the workplace, and the other is the tendency for work to creep its way into the home.

WORK CREEP SYNDROME

The term "work creep" isn't about a creepy person at work—at least, not the way I'll use it here. It describes the way that your work life can worm its way into your personal and family life. Sometimes the expectation that you should be available to your job are imposed from outside by a corporate policy or an overeager manager. Sometimes they come from an internal desire to be the best, work the hardest, and take every chance to gain a competitive edge. Sure, work has always managed to creep its way into your home life; in the past you could bring home a report and work on it. Today your laptop computer makes it possible to bring home *all* of your work, not just one report. Even your smartphone lets you access work documents from anywhere that are stored in the Cloud. And therein lies the first danger of technology creeping into your home life.

SMARTPHONES

With the advent of the mobile phone, a whole new paradigm was created regarding traditional work/home boundaries. Now your boss or anyone else at the office could get a hold of you directly when you are out of the office without the risk of one of your family members answering the call. Even worse, if your company provided the cell phone to you, as far as they are concerned it is fair game to contact you 24/7.

Then the BlackBerry came along, followed quickly by smartphones such as iPhones and Androids. E-mails are now at your fingertips, and you're expected to respond immediately. Text messaging with its (hopefully) silent, instantaneous expectations has upped the ante yet again. Saturday night at the theater, no problem. Your phone's on silent ring, but you can go to the lobby and shoot a quick text back to your boss. And if you don't, she'll want to know why.

Don't think these expectations will stop with e-mail and texting. Last night I had a call with my cousin Lizzie. As we started talking, she hit the FaceTime button on her iPhone. Suddenly I had a request to make our call a video chat.

Video can certainly add to the quality of our phone conversations. When all you have is the words typed on a screen you can miss the nonverbal facial clues that can help you understand what is being said. The video call helps give you those clues. But there's also a danger.

Consider the employee who has called in sick and is really at a ball game. It's the eighth inning, bases are loaded, and his team's best hitter is at the plate. The hitter takes a vicious cut at the first pitch: strike one. That's when the employee feels his phone ring; he pulls it out and answers it only to hear his boss on the other end and a request pops up on his screen asking to engage in a FaceTime call.

What does he do?

If he doesn't accept the request, the boss is going to wonder what's going on. If he does accept it, the boss is going to wonder why all those people behind the employee are sitting on his sick bed.

And all the boss wants to know is where to find a report the "sick" employee had forgotten to drop onto the server from home the night before. What a potentially miserable situation!

WORK CREEP: TAKING STOCK

The best place to begin managing the extent to which work is following you into your personal life is with a critical self-evaluation. Make note of:

- When and where you carry your mobile device.

- How often and in what locations you find yourself "just checking" business e-mail.

- The frequency and duration of the times that you engage in work-related activities while you are away from work.

Work creep isn't just about working too much. It's about how that extra time spent attending to work in the "off" hours affects the people in your personal life. So be willing to look at yourself as others do, and ask yourself the following questions. (If you find yourself making excuses for yourself as you read these, put them to someone very close to you):

- Are you always on the phone or replying to e-mail for work (or is that the impression you give)?

- Are you good at getting back to people in your personal life?

- Are you good at committing to uninterrupted time with family and friends?

SETTING BOUNDARIES

Just by recognizing yourself in any of these behaviors you will have taken the first step toward reducing work creep in your life. Then the steps to address the issue are simple:

- Keep "home" office hours: stay away from work devices before breakfast and after dinner.

- Consciously compartmentalize everything you have to do. For instance, when it's lunchtime, give yourself permission to enjoy your lunch.

- Carve out times in the day or week when you can give your complete attention to something not work related: sports, a date, a good book, volunteer work.

- Establish limits with your colleagues and your boss. What are reasonable hours for your manager to expect you to be available? What if it's a client or colleague? Is the standard any different for text messages or e-mails?

BREAKING HABITS

All of your life you've been programmed to answer a phone when it rings. It's no wonder that when your mobile phone rings while you're talking to your friend you instinctively reach into your pocket and answer it. Unfortunately, this habit no longer serves you well and it needs to be replaced with a different habit, one that has you assess your situation before automatically answering your phone. Places to think twice first before you answer:

- In a meeting

- At the theater

- In a restaurant

- On public transportation

- In bed

THE TIDE TURNS

The balance may be shifting. Consider new policies instituted at Volkswagen in Germany. There, some workers complained that work-related e-mails were seriously encroaching on their home lives. The solution? Servers stop routing work e-mail to employees' mobile devices or laptops thirty minutes after their shifts end, and begin routing again thirty minutes before their shifts start. While this policy only applies to Volkswagen workers under union contract in German factories, it's a good start.

LIFE CREEP

"Life creep" is the other side of the work-creep coin. Just as new technology and communication methods have allowed work life to bleed into private time and spaces, so too have they allowed private life to intrude on work. For example: a quick check on kids or elderly parents; making doctor appointments for a sick spouse; serving on a charitable board; arranging a wedding; making plans with friends; checking a grocery list with your spouse. Some companies go so far as to restrict access from work computers to social networking pages like Facebook, and others don't allow any mobile or smartphone use during work hours. At the Emily Post Institute, we allow both, but require that employees manage their time to get their work done well and on schedule. Either way, know your employer's policy for personal calls, texts, and Internet use, and follow them. Some potential trouble spots include:

- Smartphones. Personal calls circumvent the office phone (on which the disruption is more likely to be noticed), and text messages can quickly bridge the gap from the occasional to the constant. Texting can also happen without being noticed by colleagues or managers. When your cell phone rings and you answer it, people can see and hear that what you are doing isn't business. But when your friend texts you about where to watch tonight's ball game, you can answer without anyone knowing you aren't doing your work. Limit your texting to break time and at lunch.

- Social networking (aka "social *not*-working"). Social networking can serve work purposes, but it can also suck productivity out of an organization when it's about your personal life. If social media is part of your job responsibility, keep it to work-related interactions instead of making it an opportunity to comment on your friends' wall posts or watch videos they have posted.

- Web surfing. The sheer scale of the Internet allows for distractions in the workplace that were simply unimaginable even a decade ago. Gaming, shopping, news media—there's no place on the Internet that hasn't been visited on the company dime. Companies are fighting back by keeping track of where employees go on the Internet on company time.

- E-mail. The best way to protect your personal e-mails from being part of your business computer is to maintain separate e-mail accounts. It doesn't matter what provider you use, just be sure your personal account is distinct from your company account.

NSFW = NTT

When I was a child, my mother would say "N-T-T," meaning Not Table Talk, when I strayed into topics inappropriate for the dinner table. Web content that may not be appropriate for the workplace will sometimes be labeled "NSFW"—Not Safe for Work. Take the hint, and leave this material for your personal time, and don't forward NSFW material to work colleagues or associates.

LIMITING LIFE CREEP

When thinking about how to minimize life creep, it is a good idea to:

- Check your workplace policy on the above listed issues. Oftentimes, professional consequences follow abuse of company time and policies, so it is a good idea to know what the official boundaries are and stick to them.

- Take your calls in a private place. If you do need to make or answer a personal call, go to a private place where you can do it without affecting colleagues around you.

- Limit your calls. Taking a call once in a while is probably OK, but your business image could suffer if you become known as "that guy who's always on his cell phone."

- Consider having two ringtones: one for personal contacts and the other for business contacts. Then, while you are at work, send calls that ring as a personal call to voice mail.

- Tell people not to call you at work unless there is an emergency. If necessary, spell out what an emergency is, especially with kids.

- Respond to nonbusiness texts only during break times. Let your friends and family know that if they text you, you will answer them when it is convenient for you and not necessarily right away.

- Limit checking Facebook, Twitter, Tumblr, Pinterest, favorite blogs, or any other personal social media interests to breaks or lunch.

13

TOUGH TIMES

While I was writing this chapter, a close friend lost his father unexpectedly and turned to social media for support in a way that pleasantly surprised me. He is a classically taciturn and reserved New Englander. A civil engineer by trade, he has always preferred the simplicity of physics to the complexities of human emotions. The sudden death of his father was a shocking blow, and I found myself wondering how this gentle giant would cope.

At first, I was a bit surprised that he posted a status update on Facebook the next day, saying his father had passed away. He had always been just a bit of a contrarian and usually avoided Facebook. Yet this was how he chose to tell the world about his loss. I was amazed at how well it worked for him. While he was not particularly fond of keeping up correspondence or even just calling to socialize, he had a network of friends and associates across three states who were touched to learn about his loss.

Facebook allowed him to share the news of his father's death without a complicated set of calls and social interactions weighing on him. The response from his extended friend network both online and off was substantial. People replied with comments, wall posts, and more personal messages as well as with the traditional visits, phone calls, and cards. Over the next several weeks I found him checking his page often, clearly finding comfort in the connections it helped him to make.

As the days went by, both friends and family used Facebook to share photos. One picture in particular of my friend and his father showing them sporting similar outfits and beards and sitting next to each other made me smile. It quickly became a favorite item on his wall, a tribute to my friend as his father's son, with friends and family commenting on how the two of them were so clearly cut from the same cloth.

How we face challenges and difficulties in life says as much about our character as how we handle success. There are going to be times when we all face the difficulty of a disease or the death of a loved one. In these moments of loss and challenge, digital media has become part of the fabric of our tough times too.

ILLNESS

A number of online services are now available to help friends and families manage care for those who are sick or chronically ill. Long hospital stays and home health care require a great deal from family, friends, and respite-care providers. Managing visiting hours, patient care, patient meals, and a thousand other details can be ameliorated with the help of online services.

Being ill and in the hospital can be isolating for the patient. Services like CaringBridge.com, MyLifeLine.org, and CarePages.com provide a way for patients, families, and friends to offer encouragement and a network of support. It relieves families from the exhausting and time-consuming task of delivering the same news over and over. Some hospitals and care facilities maintain their own community sites and care portals. In general these sites keep patients connected to their families and friends while in the hospital and during recovery. They provide a place for guests to register and leave messages for or share photos with the patient, as well as a way for family to leave updates on the patient's progress.

Facilitating access to the Internet for those who are bedridden is another way to provide comfort. If a friend or family member is fighting an illness or is laid up with an injury, thinking about ways to give them access to the world of online connectivity is a great way to offer support. This could mean:

- Lending a laptop, tablet, or even desktop computer.

- Setting up a temporary wireless network or finding a way to access an existing home or hospital network.

- Purchasing a temporary Internet plan for a home or residence that doesn't usually have this type of service.

OLD-SCHOOL FACE TIME

There's no question that online support networks are a great help to patients and families, but don't let them be a substitute for good old-fashioned face-to-face visits. Unless you live far away, online visits shouldn't be your only contact with your friend. Make a phone call or schedule a visit as part of your support effort.

> ### Take Extra Care Responding to Bad News
>
> It is normal, natural, and admirable to want to wish a sick friend well, but be careful that you aren't the one to inadvertently spread the news of an illness to your social network. Unless your friend has revealed his condition in a public post, send these thoughts privately.

WHAT DO I SAY?

Most of us get a bit tongue-tied or word-challenged with friends who have a serious illness or injury. While our intent is to be comforting or encouraging, sometimes it's expressed awkwardly. Here are a few clichés to avoid:

- "I know how you feel." (You probably don't!)

- "You're going to be fine." (Are you the doctor?)

- "It's not that bad." (Well, now *you* feel better!)

Instead, try to think of empathetic ways to express your concern that give your friend an opportunity to express how he feels about it.

- "It must be tough."

- "I'm so sorry you're going through this."

- "I'm thinking of you."

In general:

- Don't trivialize the illness.

- Don't relate scary stories about "an uncle who died from the same thing."

- Don't go on about your own aches and pains in an attempt to relate.

- Don't dramatize how everyone else is coping (or not).

How Can I Help?

One of the first responses to news of an illness or injury is "How can I help?" Most of us have meals and visits in mind. While well-meaning and completely appropriate, it often falls to the family to organize who's bringing what or visiting when—another stressful task.

Online services such as mealTrain.com and CareCalendar.org allow friends and family to sign up for a visit or a meal. Family can control rest time, and friends can make sure that the patient isn't inundated with tuna casserole. Taking it another step, using a calendar site can also let friends know what other ways they could lend a hand, such as picking up kids from school, dropping off dry cleaning, or exchanging library books. It's brilliant, and a tremendous help to immediate caregivers.

Health Care in the Information Age

Online research about health issues using resources like Web MD (WebMD.com) and the American Cancer Society website (Cancer.org) has become a standard part of patient-directed care in the Internet age. In the same way that the Emily Post Institute advises a traveler to do a basic amount of research about a country before traveling there, it is advisable to do a minimal amount of research about a health condition in coordination with visiting a doctor. With so much information available, it makes sense that patients would take the initiative to learn about all the best ways to support the care that a doctor recommends and advises. You can never replace all of the years of training and experience that a health-care practitioner brings, but you can do some homework to be the best patient that you can be.

DIGITAL DETAILS AT THE TIME OF DEATH

There are many traditions that relate to death, condolences, and grief. These are framed by religion, culture, community, and even personal preference. Somehow the very idea of using the Internet as a relevant and helpful tool at such a personal time can seem improbable. Yet the Internet has proved to be of great benefit to families and friends who have lost a loved one. Let's see how our digital devices and online sharing can be used considerately and respectfully.

"I'M SORRY TO TELL YOU . . ."

It's never easy to tell a friend or relative that someone close to them has died. As important as the words you use is the way you let someone know. My friend did a great job using Facebook to let his wider circle of friends know of his loss. But what about telling close family members, such as parents, grandparents, siblings, aunts, and uncles? Immediate family and very close friends should, whenever possible, receive the news personally, either face-to-face or with a phone call. If you cannot reach someone, leave a message or send an e-mail without delivering the actual news: "It's Jeff; please call me as soon as you can. It's important." This type of message still gives you the opportunity to be present with the person when you deliver the news. How would you feel if you learned your dad died from your cousin's Facebook page, a voice mail, or an e-mail? Do all you can to deliver sad news as personally as possible.

How Soon Should You Mention a Death on a Social Network?

It is critical to give a family enough time to notify other family and close friends personally. It is OK to post the news a few days later, or after the obituary or death notice has appeared in the newspaper or online. If you have any doubts, ask a principal family member.

OBITUARIES, REMEMBRANCES, AND SUPPORT

Online obituary and remembrance books are often components of the contemporary funeral process. Many people find these tools to be a creative and meaningful way to memorialize the departed. In fact, some services offer to build digital profiles of the deceased, similar to a social network page. Here are some options to consider:

- Online obituaries. The common elements of a traditional printed obituary are also included in an online obituary: name, date of birth and death, work or professional accomplishments, personal achievements, amateur passions, and surviving family. Some newspapers offer the online version for free; there is usually a per-word or per-line charge for the printed version. Many newspapers use Legacy.com for the online obituary so readers from different places can access it. If you're the one organizing the obituary, be sure to let the immediate family know about this online memorial.

- Online remembrance books. An online guest book or remembrance page is often included with the online obituary. Consider offering thoughts of condolence for those who remain instead of directing your comments to the deceased (for example, avoid things like "Buddy, I know you're in a better place"). Go ahead and share your thoughts and feelings about the deceased if you feel so inclined. But remember your post is public, so don't reveal anything best kept private. Families also use these guest books to post information about the upcoming service or to post a general thanks to all who signed in.

- Support services. There are a host of informational and support services that are available online as well. Websites such as Heart2Soul.com provide resources for funeral planning as well as expert advice and forums to help the grieving cope. There are forums designed to bring people together who are facing similar difficulties. Also available are online services specific to certain faiths or to deaths caused by a particular illness, such as cancer, which can be especially helpful and are potentially a great source of information and community support in a time of need.

LIVING WILL 2.0

Many people can barely keep track of their own passwords and online accounts, so imagine trying to figure out someone else's network when their help is no longer available. The process of shutting down a digital profile for an individual who has died can be a complicated and time-consuming process.

- Living wills should include directions for accessing and closing social network contacts and accounts as well as any online business accounts. While a person's page may be closed, information and photos that have spread will live on. Make it a point to update and print out a list of all your online passwords or access codes on a regular basis and file it in a secure place or with the person to whom you have given power of attorney.

- Leave instructions for shutting down any automated content, such as preloaded Twitter feeds and blog posts.

- Be sure the person to whom you have given power of attorney has lists of all online or pay-for accounts and that they have the access permissions to make any required changes.

Ghosts in the Machine

One unanticipated consequence of social networking is that images of people who have died outlive the people they represent. Data associated with a certain person can spread out and occupy so many locations that it may be impossible to remove all traces even if you wished to do so after the person has died. Some even think of these lingering digital reflections as a new type of ghost.

It can be unsettling to first encounter this while in the state of emotional upheaval that is usually a part of the grieving process. The time immediately after someone has died can be confusing and emotionally fraught. Facebook pages and Twitter accounts with automated feeds may continue to appear active after someone is gone. For example, birthday alerts sent from unmanaged Facebook profiles of the departed are an increasingly common occurrence. These digital ripples in the pool of the World Wide Web are often observed months and even years after someone dies. This echo phenomenon can be disconcerting for someone still receiving notifications from a deceased friend or loved one.

An ounce of prevention can go a long way toward curbing the upset that these events can cause. Just being aware that a digital ghost may linger for a period of time can help avoid the shock that an encounter with this information can cause.

If you do receive a Facebook notice—such as a birthday alert—consider turning it into a positive by making a post saying how nice it is to have the opportunity to remember someone and what a wonderful person he was.

VISITING HOURS AND FUNERALS

Visiting the family before the funeral or attending the funeral itself are times when being respectful is paramount. One way to show respect is to be fully present, and that means limiting any possibility of distraction. Unless you're on-call, power off all digital devices before you visit with the family or attend the funeral. Ringers and text alerts have no place here and can trivialize the solemnity of the occasion. It would be highly disrespectful to tweet from a funeral, or, worse, take photos of the deceased or the family.

OFFERING CONDOLENCES

Because condolences are so personal, there is no set form, but let one simple rule guide you: say what you truly feel. A single sincere line expressing your feelings about the deceased or sharing a specific memory is all you need to say. Whether in person or in writing, don't dwell on the details of the illness or the manner of death, and don't say things like "He's in a better place," or "It's a blessing in disguise."

E-mails, texts, online remembrance books, and social network posts are all ways to give immediate support to family and friends. If you have a long or very personal message, e-mail is a more private option than a public post. But don't let your online post keep you from making more personal contacts. If you can, do make the effort to visit the family or attend the service; otherwise, in the weeks to come, consider following up your digital delivery with a phone call or handwritten note.

ACKNOWLEDGING CONDOLENCES

After the funeral, families acknowledge flowers, donations, notes, calls, and kindnesses with a personal note of thanks and appreciation. But how do you respond to the perhaps hundreds of online posts and messages? Think of it this way: Respond using the same medium. It's perfectly fine to post a general message of thanks to all those who signed an online remembrance book or social-network page. While it is not necessary to respond to e-mails or texts of the "so sorry for your loss" variety, do reply personally to anyone who wrote a more personal message.

14

DIGITAL SAFETY

When your guest is about to try and drive home drunk and won't take a subtle hint, you should take his keys—even if he finds it offensive. Everyone knows this. Safety is a priority above etiquette, and that's true online as well as off. While online safety is not the topic of this book, I can't really talk about the best ways to engage the online world without also addressing personal safety. Once you become dependent on computers and mobile devices, it's important to take the necessary steps to protect your information, privacy, and passwords. In this chapter we'll look into how to do that and how to avoid online scams, protect your devices, and avoid viruses. Finally, we'll look at the dangers of using your mobile device while driving.

INTERNET SAFETY

Online safety, above all, is about using good judgment and making safe behaviors a habit. As a part of being online you have a responsibility to stay current in order to keep you and your information safe and private.

BE DISCREET

Discretion is the better part of valor, and it can help protect you too. Learning to use discretion online is a critically important part of operating in such a public environment.

- A home address, for example, should be closely guarded and given out only with great care. Be aware that photos of your home, or taken at your home, may contain location information that could give away your residential address.

- Think about how much personal information you give out in early conversations or e-mail exchanges with people you meet online. Be as careful with details about the lives of friends, coworkers, and family as you would with your own.

- Review what your personal information limits are before you get drawn past them by an unexpected question or turn in a conversation.

- Be extra-careful with sensitive business and financial information.

- Keep pictures of children "privacy protected" if you share them with friends and family.

STAY ON GUARD FOR ONLINE SCAMS

We have all seen it: The e-mail that looks like it is from your friend down the hall at work telling you he is in a foreign country and has lost his wallet and all his documents. All he needs is for you to send him some money really quick so he can get some food and a flight home. The next e-mail you see from him is one explaining that his account was hacked and he is hoping that you didn't send any money yet because he is still very much just down the hall at his desk.

Stay vigilant. Keep your good-sense radar up; it is your best defense. Remember the old saying, "If it seems too good to be true, it probably is." These are a few of the common online trouble areas today:

- **Scams that use your current e-mail and social media contact lists.** One scam mimics e-mails or messages sent from social-media accounts asking for help, money, or valuable information. By using current contact lists, the scams come from e-mail addresses you would recognize as trusted, so never send or wire money unless you are sure of the recipient and have independently verified their situation.

- **Scams that target seniors, recent immigrants, and dating-site members.** These groups should stay especially alert as scams specifically directed at them are designed to be very personal and to push specific emotional buttons.

- **Scams designed to facilitate identity theft.** It is important to protect your identity by keeping your full name, Social Security number, bank information, passwords, and even certain e-mails private. This will help to avoid most common phishing scams; ploys designed to steal from you by acquiring personal information that would allow access to your accounts.

The "Rule of Too" Works Online, Too

Remember the "Rule of Too." If you find yourself asking, "Is this is too much?" or "Am I going too far?" then you should proceed with caution. Trust your own good judgment and common sense and pull back before you can't take it back.

MEETING OFFLINE

Meeting people online sometimes leads to an in-person encounter, an exchange of goods or services, or even an online job. It is only natural as more and more people interact successfully online that actual meetings become more commonplace. It is precisely because there is such a general acceptance of web-based socializing that it is necessary to review how to safely move a relationship from the virtual world to the real world.

These rules apply to any situation when people who have met online are meeting for the first time. Maybe you are planning on attending your first political event organized by your favorite local political blog. Or perhaps you are going to the midnight showing of a new movie with a sci-fi fan club organized on Facebook. You might be joining your online gaming club's monthly trip to the nearby casino, or maybe you are simply meeting someone to pick up an item you purchased on Craigslist. Anytime you step out into a new situation with people who you have met online, it is a good idea to build a safety net.

MAKE IT PUBLIC

When you meet an online contact in person for the first time, there are several things you should do:

- Make first contact in a well-lit, well-traveled public place, such as a coffee shop or park.

- When it comes to friendship or dating, not every encounter will satisfy expectations. Keep first meetings short, and have your own way to get home.

- Make a first encounter a group event to get to know new people in the relative safety of a more social situation. Barbecues, art galleries, sporting events, flea markets, and farmers' markets can all be great venues to meet at for the first time.

- Make sure that someone you trust knows what you are doing, who you are with, where you are, and when you are expected to be back or to check in.

Decide ahead of time what actions your safety-check friend should take if they don't hear from you.

VERIFY

Trade some information with the person you are meeting that verifies their identity. You can protect yourself from many layers of deception by taking this simple precaution. Verify enough information to be reasonably assured that they are being honest in how they represent themselves. This could be as simple as looking them up in the phonebook, verifying that their employer does indeed exist and employ them, or doing a Google search about the person. For many established community sites, a profile name from an account with a solid user history is enough of a background check to proceed with a meeting, but when using open forums like Craigslist or Yahoo! Personals, checking someone's personal information is an important part of the safety process before you meet.

A great clue as to someone's trustworthiness is the degree to which they operate alone. Networks of friends, family, and coworkers are harder to manipulate than words typed on a chat site and offer clues as to how truthful someone is being in how they represent themselves. Do they really have a sister? (Yes, there she is on Facebook with photos and wall posts.) The movie *Catfish* hinges on the inherent drama involved in staging a fake life online, but only in Hollywood is this level of deception truly possible. While single people and solo operators are obviously not all untrustworthy, take a slower and more careful approach with someone who doesn't seem to be connected to any kind of community.

GPS: Can You See Me Now?

There are more and more mobile and social media services using real-time global positioning software (GPS) to connect people who are currently in the same city, neighborhood, or even building. For example, Foursquare and Twitter can tell others where you are, and applications such as RunKeeper keep a record of all your runs or walks, including route, time, and distance information. While the possibilities this opens up are exciting, the safety concerns involved in using services and devices that link you to your real-time location are complex and very real. Think carefully about how you will use it before you employ any of these services. They are best used in a group or among friends.

The Buddy System

The buddy system has worked well for scuba divers, soldiers, mountain climbers, and in all manner of extreme situations. It can work for the brave new world of GPS-empowered mobile technology and social software as well. When we venture into unknown conditions and there is the potential for danger, there is no protection that can replace the value of a second set of eyes.

When you are with friends it might be fun to turn on your GPS feature to share your location with everybody who is at the same concert or sporting event as you. But when you leave the protective company of your friends, turn it off. If the GPS is still on while you're traveling home, someone could use it to track your movements, follow you home, or figure out where you live. So, turn it on when you want to use it and remember to turn it off when you're done.

Safety Apps

A world of increased connectivity may open up some new vulnerabilities, but it also offers new protections. There is a whole suite of apps available for mobile devices that offer safety features for the mobile-phone user, such as emergency notification of 911 in the case of an accident or anytime/anywhere security advice from law enforcement professionals. Wireless home security cameras can be accessed from any web browser with the right software, and home alarms can be monitored from the office or ballpark.

PROTECT YOURSELF AND YOUR DEVICES

The first step in protecting your information is to physically keep track of your devices. Consider using a permanent marker, business card, or label maker to discreetly label your device—say, under the hard case of your smartphone or on the underside of your laptop—with a return address, e-mail, and maybe even an offer of a small reward for its safe return should you lose or misplace it. A sticker, label, or permanent mark can be all you need to identify your laptop from the thousands of others that look just like it in the airport security screening bins. It could save you from having to replace a costly device or compromising any confidential information stored on it. Some devices have location services that can tell you where they are, as well as lock them remotely or even send a message to whomever finds them. It is worth taking the time to learn how to use these features.

PASSWORDS

When I give business seminars, I often ask my audience, "If someone stole or found your phone, would that person be able to access your business e-mail account?" When the answer is "Yes," as it often is, it is time to password-protect that device or account.

Sensitive information stored on work devices presents its own set of dilemmas. Extra precautions need to be taken with laptops, tablets, and phones that hold e-mails or documents containing confidential business information, and credit card or Social Security numbers. Having strong password protection for sensitive information is a must for responsible device use. Keep these points in mind as you manage your passwords and password-protected accounts:

- Use passwords. Don't assume you are safe or will never be hacked.

- Use different passwords for different things. I know this is annoying, but don't use the same password for Facebook, your bank account, your work e-mail, and your fantasy football league.

- Use at least mildly original words and combinations of words and numbers to build your passwords. "Princess(your name)," your birth date, and "abcdefg" are the first options that hackers try.

- The more sensitive the information, the more complicated the password. Use a case-sensitive combination of letters, numbers, and symbols for better security.

- The best protection against hackers is to use a complete sentence as a password. If the site will allow it, pick a favorite line from a book or movie that you will never forget—but again, avoid the most obvious: "tobeornottobethatisthequestion."

- Keep track of all your different passwords and accounts using a cheat sheet or password-management program such as oneSafe or Pin Vault to which only you and one other trusted person have access.

VIRUSES

Computers can get sick, just like people. Preventing the spread of computer viruses is an important part of being a good online citizen. Just as you keep your hands clean to protect yourself, you want to keep your computer clean as well. Few things are as frustrating as fighting a virus that disrupts your computer's function. Even worse are the viruses that you don't know you have and that can spread rapidly as they work in the background of your computer or device. Some viruses use your computer to send spam e-mails from your accounts as if it were you doing it. You could have no way of knowing this is happening until you hear from your e-mail provider that you have been labeled a spammer and blocked by all the major e-mail providers. So what can you do to protect yourself?

- Keep operating systems, software, and antivirus programs up to date.

- Be careful about what you download online. Don't download anything from a website that you don't have good reason to know and trust (such as the official site for a piece of software that needs regular updating).

- Never open executable files (labeled .exe) that you receive in e-mails! These files launch (execute) programs on your computer and can be among the quickest ways to catch a virus.

- In fact, don't open any files from people you don't know. If you have a question about an attachment sent by someone you trust, just confirm that it really is from her—and not someone who hacked her mail—before you open it.

- As a general rule, don't open e-mails that don't have a subject line.

BACKUP, BACKUP, BACKUP

Part of feeling confident and secure in digital spaces is being comfortable that the things you value are protected. The music stored on your computer, the photos taken on your smartphone, and the home videos burned on CDs all need to be protected and backed up.

- **Redundancy is important.** Have more than one storage system and think about keeping them in different places. It does you no good to have several hard-drive backups that are all in the same closet when a pipe bursts in the bathroom above.

- **Test it!** You don't know how good your backup system is until you put away your current devices and try to recover your data from scratch.

- **Update formats as technology changes.** For example, if you use a camera that only works with a certain computer or piece of software, pay attention so you will know if the manufacturer plans to stop supporting that format or device. Then you can take the appropriate steps to update the format or purchase new hardware.

- **Learn to use the Cloud**. Cloud memory, or wireless network storage, can make it easier to back up data by reducing the need to plug in external devices. Just be sure you know where it is stored and how to get it back.

DRIVING SAFELY

Chocolate and peanut butter; kittens and yarn; Calvin and Hobbes—some things just go together.

Oil and water, bulls and china shops, texting and driving—some things just don't.

Shortly after graduating from college, I returned home and visited the family doctor for a physical. Our doctor was a pleasant family practitioner who had known me since I was a young boy. After a brief checkup, he finished with three pieces of advice for the next ten years of my life, advice that I took to heart: have fun, don't take up smoking, and be sure to wear my seat belt every time I got in the car. His point: the biggest dangers that I faced over the next ten years would be acquiring a smoking habit that I could not shake or dying in a car accident.

For a great many people, the most dangerous act they engage in daily is driving or riding in a car. Despite efforts to develop viable public transit options, cars are an almost unavoidable component of contemporary American life. In fact, so much so that we sometimes forget the power of the automobile. An internal combustion engine controlling the explosion of vaporized gasoline, hurtling several tons of metal, plastic, and glass down the road at speeds many times natural maximum human velocity is one of the great marvels of the twentieth century. But in the blink of an eye, you can be seriously injured. Driving is a serious responsibility and safety must be a foremost concern.

WHAT IS DISTRACTING?

Someone I know well, who will remain nameless, used to write notes to herself while driving to work. She used to do it one-handed on a pad of paper she kept on the passenger seat. She claimed that she never even looked down at the paper, and the notes read like a cross between abstract art and brainstorming charts. When I showed her a simple-to-use voice-to-text app for her phone, I know I did a service for commuters in her community. Now she happily records the same notes on her way to work without me having to worry about a ten-car pileup on the interstate.

And therein lies the conundrum we face today about using communication technology while driving. People used to say radios in cars were a danger. Perhaps they are, but would we give them up? State legislatures haven't finished resolving current questions about what is and what is not "distracting." Some states have laws prohibiting the use of hand-held phones but allow hands-free operation. Others ban both hand-held and hands-free. Still others have no laws on the books at all.

The National Transportation Safety Board will tell you that any use of a mobile phone is a distraction, hands-free or not. And there is certainly logic to that argument. When you drive by me at sixty miles per hour in the opposite direction, I'd like to think that you are 100 percent focused on the road and me—not on what your boyfriend, girlfriend, significant other, parent, sibling, friend, client, or anyone else has just said on the phone.

THE FACTS DON'T LIE

Despite our desire to think of ourselves as highly capable multitaskers, studies show that distractions while driving are dangerous and lead to increased rates of accidents and driving-related injuries and death. It's little wonder that more and more states are outlawing texting while driving.

The smartphone is just the latest intrusion into the car environment that can be a distraction to the driver. A study conducted by the Texas Transportation Institute found that 25 percent of all fatal crashes are directly related to driver distraction. Research from Virginia Tech went further:

- Whether cell phones are used for conversation or other visual tasks, they are the single most common source of distraction.

- When used for texting messages, cell phones are thought to increase the fatal crash risk six to 23 times over the baseline.

- 20 percent of drivers in 2009 admitted to texting while driving.

TEN TIPS FOR MANAGING DRIVER DISTRACTIONS

Distracted drivers pose a deadly risk to everyone on the road. Here are ten tips from the Governors Highway Safety Association for managing some of the most common distractions.

1. **Turn it off.** Turn off your phone or switch to silent mode before you get in the car.

2. **Spread the word.** Set up a special message to tell callers that you are driving and you'll get back to them as soon as possible, or sign up for a service that does this.

3. **Pull over.** If you need to make a call, pull over to a safe area first.

4. **Use your passengers.** Ask a passenger to make the call for you.

5. **X the Text.** Don't *ever* text and drive, surf the web, or read your e-mail while driving. It is dangerous and against the law in most states.

6. **Know the law.** Familiarize yourself with state and local laws before you get in the car. Some states and localities prohibit the use of hand-held cell phones. GHSA offers a handy chart of state laws on its website: www.ghsa.org/html/stateinfo/laws/cellphone_laws.html.

7. **Prepare.** Review maps and directions before you start to drive. If you need help when you are on the road, ask a passenger to help or pull over to a safe location to review the map/directions again.

8. **Secure your pets.** Pets can be a big distraction in the car. Always secure your pets properly before you start to drive.

9. **Keep the kids safe.** Pull over to a safe location to address situations with your children.

10. **Focus on the task at hand.** Refrain from smoking, eating, drinking, reading, and any other activity that takes your mind and eyes off the road.

The Law

Many states have passed laws about use of cell phones while driving. Some have expanded the focus to include laws against texting while driving. Consult your secretary of state to inquire about current laws in your area. You are responsible for knowing about these laws in the same way you are responsible for having proper insurance and for obeying the speed limit. If you plan to travel and intend to use your mobile device while driving, check on laws for the states that you will be traveling in, as they are not necessarily all the same.

TEXTING: NOT AN "LOL" MATTER

There is simply no safe way to text while driving.

If your eyes are on a keypad, they aren't on the road. If you're thinking about what to write, you're not thinking about what's ahead of you. Think you can look away and be distracted for just a few seconds? Think again. At fifty miles per hour you'll go 315 feet in just three seconds—that's more than the length of a football field. You take a lot longer than three seconds to read, much less write, a text message.

Cell phone records at the time of an accident may be subpoenaed as part of an accident investigation. A train engineer who was focused on his texting ran a red signal and crashed head-on into an oncoming train. They know he was texting at the moment of impact by the record of his texts.

E-mail, Twitter, and Instant Messaging are just as dangerous, of course. The difference between checking and responding to e-mails, IMs, or tweets on a mobile device and texting are negligible and a matter of semantics at best. If it's really so important, please pull over somewhere safe and take care of it from the safety of a parked car. The life you save could be your own, but it could also be the innocent person in another car.

NAVIGATION SYSTEMS

Navigation apps are great; the key is to be smart about how you use them.

- Know your system. Practice and try out new features on familiar roads and routes. The time to learn is not in an unfamiliar city during rush hour when you are late for a flight.

- Before you start out, put the parameters for your trip into the device and review your route.

- Don't trust the machine more than your good sense. Roads change with work and the seasons. Certain routes are affected by traffic at certain times of day. No map is perfect, even the digital one that can talk to you.

- When in doubt, pull over—just as you should with that hard-copy map. Safety comes first. Your destination is not likely to go anywhere.

- If you are getting help from a navigator, spend a few minutes setting them up to help you before you depart.

Not all navigation systems are created equal. If you have one that has voice commands and a display that is designed for a driver, these tools can equip you to drive safely. But a smartphone that requires two hands to operate and has screen that you need to hold close to your face and pinch and pull at to see should never be used while driving.

PASSENGER DOS

A gracious heart is at the center of all good manners. Anytime you can help to make someone else's life a little easier, go for it. Who wouldn't like to hear "Can I help keep an eye out for our exit?" Here are a few passenger dos.

- Offer to help navigate. A second set of eyes can be very useful to a driver trying to find her way.

- Offer to manage the radio, navigation system, or to make and answer any necessary calls.

- While it's not about safety, helping to pay for gas is an often unexpected but almost always appreciated gesture, especially with today's prices.

THE DIGITAL DOWNLOAD

In the rapidly changing world of the Internet and mobile communications it can seem as if common courtesies and civil behavior are being left behind. But they don't need to be. By being thoughtful and considerate in our actions we can promote civil behaviors in the online world just as we do in person. Fundamentally, etiquette really is about how we treat people, no matter what we are doing—or where, when, or with whom we are doing it. That is what truly matters.

Manners do change and evolve over time, and social media is still a bit of a new frontier. This can be seen in the way new laws and customs are being tested and accepted or discarded. Yet as each day passes, the manners surrounding the ways we use technology and how we communicate are being more firmly established. What will come next? Your guess is as good as mine. What we know for sure is that while technology will change again, and new manners will evolve, these fundamentals will serve you well as you venture forth in this brave new online and mobile world.

Social-Media and Mobile-Device Fundamentals

If you ever find yourself unsure of what to do in the virtual world or when using your mobile device, remember these points to be sure you are behaving well.

The Dinner-Table Rule

People identify the dinner table as the most civil place in their lives. Sure, it's where we share food with others, but it's also where we build relationships with people who are important to us. Because it is a place that many associate with civil conduct, it is a great frame of reference for assessing and moderating online behaviors. What you do online reflects back on you. It can seem like another, more anonymous, world, where extreme behaviors and ideas are the norm. However, you are just as responsible for what you say and do there as in the physical world you inhabit. Ask yourself: "Would I do or say this at the dinner table?" as a reminder of this fact.

As a way to help moderate your choices, picture someone whose opinion matters to you—your parents, your children, or a mentor—observing you in a close and personal setting, such as when you are sharing a meal. When you are online, facing a question about what is appropriate to say or do, think about that person's reaction. What would they say if you brought it up the next time you shared a dinner?

Everything that happens online is in some way both public and permanent, and our actions in those spaces can have long-lasting and far-reaching effects. There is no telling when or where something done online could pop up again. Would you be comfortable if what you posted got back to your parents, spouse, or kids? What if someone put it on the bulletin board at your office? Use the "dinner-table rule" as your standard to help hold yourself accountable no matter who you are dealing with online, and the answers to these questions can be a confident "yes."

THE ILLUSION OF PRIVACY

BE CAREFUL OF PRIVATE CONVERSATION IN PUBLIC PLACES

The fact that we can communicate instantly with anyone from anywhere often creates a false sense of privacy. While your attention is focused on the person you are communicating with, don't be oblivious to who else might be privy to your communication or who else might be around. Your private conversations can easily be overheard by strangers.

BE CAREFUL OF PRIVATE CONVERSATIONS
IN VIRTUAL PUBLIC PLACES

So often we let our perception of a place as being private fool us into saying or doing something online that we shouldn't. Is your office, or your living room, or even your bedroom really private? You may think so but the reality is that the medium or device you are using makes no distinctions about privacy based on location or content. Communication in the virtual world is still potentially public and permanent, no matter the intent of the sender. Don't be seduced by the illusion of privacy.

BALANCE YOUR DIGITAL DIET

We balance our diet by eating from the rainbow or the four food groups. Our relationships require diversity and balance also. No single device or medium will be appropriate for every person or situation. Do you find yourself only communicating via e-mail at work? Are all of your interactions with friends occurring only via Facebook or texts? Take a look at your digital diet and consider rebalancing it using all of the tools available to you—text, e-mail, video, IM, and even the good old-fashioned but still much-appreciated handwritten note or card. Not to mention seeing someone in person!

OFFLINE RELATIONSHIPS: COMING FULL CIRCLE

In an increasingly connected world, it is up to each individual to set boundaries. Between work and personal lives. Between close family and friends and more casual acquaintances. Between total strangers and ourselves. Striking the balance between sharing and oversharing, staying connected and protecting privacy, giving loved ones access while retaining some personal space—these all require balancing. To do this well requires us to think about the relationships in our lives and make deliberate choices about how we want to conduct and maintain them.

At the end of the day, there are certain fundamental aspects of the human experience that simply don't change. For instance, the desire to socialize in person, or to spend time and to share the same space with one another. Despite everything you may have heard about the isolating and overwhelming effects of today's hypernetworked world, people will continue to meet face-to-face.

Sometimes it's for the sake of saving a relationship; other times it's to build one in a new and different way. However adept you become at using new media to interact with all the people in your life, it is critical to continue to spend time with people face-to-face.

In the end, the real value of using these communication tools effectively is they can enhance our relationships. If we don't use them well, they won't serve our relationships, no matter how advanced the device. If this is the case for you, it might be time to adopt some new behaviors, or modify the ones you use now. Or it might be time to simply unplug for a few hours. Remember to power down occasionally, get offline, disconnect, and breathe deeply. Step away from the hum of electricity and microchips and screens, rub your temples, and take a long stretch. Let your eyes focus on something within reach and then look at something far away and let them refocus again. Seek out the people you've been staying in touch with digitally. All of the mobile devices we use and social media sites we hang out on are great stand-ins for the real deal: but nothing beats spending time with the people who matter most to us.

So go ahead and enjoy the best of both worlds: text a friend, go meet for a coffee, turn on your favorite GPS-powered social search, and see what happens next.

cover design by Andrea C. Uva

978-1-4532-5495-0

Published in 2013 by Open Road Integrated Media
345 Hudson Street
New York, NY 10014
www.openroadmedia.com

OPEN ROAD

INTEGRATED MEDIA

Open Road Integrated Media is a digital publisher and multimedia content company. Open Road creates connections between authors and their audiences by marketing its ebooks through a new proprietary online platform, which uses premium video content and social media.

CPSIA information can be obtained at www.ICGtesting.com
Printed in the USA
BVOW100832110313

315061BV00001B/1/P

9 781453 254950